Globalization

Globalization: A Key Idea for Business and Society analyzes today's process of global integration. Globalization is seen as a complex phenomenon, the drivers of which are of a technological, institutional, cultural and, not least, political nature.

The book includes a historical analysis of the rise, and fall, of the "first globalization" wave which took place between the end of the Napoleonic Wars and the Great War. The chapters focus on the measurement of the global integration process, on the in-depth analysis of the above mentioned "drivers", and on some of the actors playing a relevant role in the process itself – multinational companies and governments as owners of global companies. The conclusion of the book provides a perspective on the current "globalization backlash", its determinants and possible future alternative scenarios.

This book is an ideal resource for students and practitioners interested in past, present and future globalization.

Veronica Binda is Lecturer in Business and Economic History at Bocconi University, Italy.

Andrea Colli is Professor of Economic History at Bocconi University, Italy.

Key Ideas in Business and Management

Edited by Stewart Clegg

Understanding how business affects and is affected by the wider world is a challenge made more difficult by the disaggregation between various disciplines, from operations research to corporate governance. This series features concise books that break out from disciplinary silos to facilitate understanding by analysing key ideas that shape and influence business, organizations and management.

Each book focuses on a key idea, locating it in relation to other fields, facilitating deeper understanding of its applications and meanings, and providing critical discussion of the contribution of relevant authors and thinkers. The books provide students and scholars with thought-provoking insights that aid the study and research of business and management.

Professions
A Key Idea for Business and Society
Mike Saks

Surveillance
A Key Idea for Business and Society
Graham Sewell

Sustainability
A Key Idea for Business and Society
Suzanne Benn, Melissa Edwards and Tim Williams

Human Rights
A Key Idea for Business and Society
Karin Buhmann

Complexity
A Key Idea for Business and Society
Chris Mowles

Power
A Key Idea for Business and Society
Reinoud Bosch

Employment
A Key Idea for Business and Society
Jamie Woodcock

Diversity
A Key Idea for Business and Society
Mustafa F. Özbilgin

Globalization
A Key Idea for Business and Society
Veronica Binda and Andrea Colli

For more information about this series, please visit: www.routledge.com/Key-Ideas-in-Business-and-Management/book-series/KEYBUS

Globalization

A Key Idea for Business and Society

Veronica Binda and Andrea Colli

Routledge
Taylor & Francis Group

LONDON AND NEW YORK

Designed cover image: joecicak

First published 2024
by Routledge
4 Park Square, Milton Park, Abingdon, Oxon OX14 4RN

and by Routledge
605 Third Avenue, New York, NY 10158

Routledge is an imprint of the Taylor & Francis Group, an informa business

© 2024 Veronica Binda and Andrea Colli

British Library Cataloguing-in-Publication Data
A catalogue record for this book is available from the British Library

ISBN: 9781138591912 (hbk)
ISBN: 9781138591929 (pbk)
ISBN: 9780429490255 (ebk)

DOI: 10.4324/9780429490255

Typeset in Perpetua
by Deanta Global Publishing Services, Chennai, India

To Giovanna and Umberto
In memory of Susanna

Contents

Chapter 1

Why (another) book about globalization?

D URING THE LAST THREE DECADES, BOOKS dealing in one way or another with globalization have progressively filled the shelves of bookstores and libraries. According to the raw data available from a very rapid consultation of Google Books Ngram Viewer (Figure 1.1), the trend is straightforward.

Books with the term "globalization" in their titles began to appear in the second half of the 1980s. The curve rose steadily over the course of the following decade, then soared from the mid-1990s to 2007–2008, arguably in coincidence with the epochal turning point represented by the global financial crisis. Since then, globalization has become a regular guest on the bookshelves, but its popularity as a subject has slowed into a relative decline. One aim of this book is to explain the reasons for this.

1.1 First reason: the global *Zeitenwende*

In a recent article (December 2022) published in the influential magazine *Foreign Affairs*, current German chancellor Olaf Scholz used the term *Zeitenwende* (turning, or better "inflection", point) to refer to the tectonic shift in the present status of the world's economic integration and its political hierarchies. The reversal in the "popularity" of globalization is the first reason for yet another book discussing the nature and structure of the process of global integration. We are, indeed, in the midst of an inflection point that affects an apparently monotonic trend towards a steadily increasing and pervasive global integration that characterized the decades from the end of the Cold War up until the global financial crisis of 2008. The first reason for writing another book about globalization is not, therefore, primarily to explain what globalization is, although this is extensively addressed in the following chapters, but rather to understand in greater detail which components of the

DOI: 10.4324/9780429490255-1

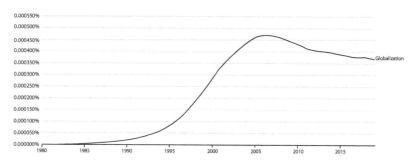

Figure 1.1 "Globalization" in book titles, 1980–2020

process have contributed to its progressive slowdown. There is compelling evidence that the next few decades will be characterized by a very different outlook. Drawing on a generalized sense of uncertainty, several commentators speak openly of "multiple alternative futures" for the current condition of globalization. One aim of this book is, therefore, to provide the reader with a suitable set of tools for better evaluation of prospects for the evolution of the present framework.

1.2 Second reason: globalization and its dark side

A second but no less important reason for writing a book like this is that, after three decades of rampant globalization, the general opinion on the phenomenon itself is quite different from the optimistic opinion generally held in the last decade of the 20th century and the first few years of the new millennium. The last ten years have progressively exposed a number of flaws in the integration process, which have opened the way toward increasing criticism. Globalization was largely based on a shared consensus that the process of global integration based upon the diffusion of liberalized free competitive markets and upon the free circulation of capital and labor would be beneficial for individuals and countries. However, these promises have encountered the reality of increasing inequality, impoverishment, uncontrolled migration flows and disruption of labor markets. This has been accompanied by a growing sense of uncertainty that has quickly turned to anger and support for anti-globalist populist movements.

However, this changing perception of globalization as a positive process is not new. In a recent compelling book with the evocative title *Against the World*, US historian Tara Zahra has vividly described how the interwar years were marked by growing hostility toward the process of global integration that occurred in the second half of the 19th century and lasted until the outbreak of the Great War in 1914. Similar dynamics are now found in the present day. The process of global integration, and especially its economic component, is coming under heavy attack. Although the positive results of globalization include some marginal countries that have rapidly modernized, raising their populations' living standards to levels previously unimaginable, what seems to prevail today is a critical view of globalization as a positive-sum game.

The global financial crisis of 2007–2008 dramatically exposed the risks of excessive liberalization and integration of the world's financial markets, bringing to a halt the enthusiastic approach of the "Washington Consensus" in the decades following the Cold War. The great crisis was quickly brought under control by remarkable international cooperation between governments and central banks, but the globalization process had certain structural endogenous flaws that soon emerged during the first two decades of the new millennium.

A profound contradiction has marked the impact of global integration on developed Western economies, and above all on their societies. First of all, globalization meant a sometimes problematic and uncontrollable trend of outsourcing and relocation of production to countries with lower costs, accompanied by a flow of low-cost products onto Western markets, facilitated by low trade barriers. For example, the average tariff on trade in 2010 was actually two-thirds lower than in 1989. This was beneficial for underdeveloped countries, but triggered a number of unintended consequences. Firstly, while income inequality *among* developed and developing countries was sharply reduced, inequality levels *inside* countries increased significantly, particularly inside what had previously been affluent Western societies. In social market Western European economies, for instance, the share of national income captured by the top 1 percent of the population rose from 10 to 12 percent between 1990 and 2020, and in the US from 14 to 20 percent. During the same period, the bottom 50 percent of Americans lost around 6 percent of their share of national income. These societies reacted bitterly. The Indian-born writer Pankaj Mishra has found an excellent term to describe the spread of rage, bitterness and malaise which characterizes our present times, using *The Age of Anger* as the title for his bestseller published in 2018. In Mishra's view, anger is not at all limited to Western societies: in its many forms and aspects, including religious violence, ethnic supremacism, and political instability, it is common to both developed and developing countries, in both the northern and southern hemispheres.

Anger takes many forms, and commonly has an impact on political preferences and voting behavior. In 1990, only four countries were governed by political coalitions in which populist parties played a relevant role; three decades later, this number had multiplied by five. Left- and right-wing populism had gained consensus from South America to the US, and increasingly within Europe. Populism's "popularity", as economists and political scientists point out, has a close relationship with rising inequality levels and the spread of anti-globalization.

Modern populism is not radically different from its interwar versions described by Zahra; it translates into the moral battleground between the uncorrupted people and the rapacious elites, and between the "national" and the "different", whether in ethnic or religious terms. It translates ultimately into an attitude that is culturally, politically and economically inward-looking. The political economy of populism is protectionist, autarchic and defensive. It opposes the dangers of uncontrolled free-market forces in the name of protection of the national economy and society.

An effective symbol of the consequences of radicalization of populist rhetoric against globalization is a famous episode that occurred during the World Economic Forum at Davos on January 2017. It was actually the autocratic leader of Communist China, Xi Jinping, who spoke out in firm defense of the liberal economic order against the dangers of trade wars and protectionism, providing a sharp contrast with the anti-globalization rhetoric of US president-elect Donald Trump.

1.3 Third reason: globalization and the return of geopolitics

The Davos episode is particularly important for another reason, which is a third motive for a more-in-depth reflection about globalization. In addition to the impact on inequality levels and the ensuing effects on voting preferences, the process of global integration following the end of the Cold War had a profound impact on the world order intended as the hierarchy of geopolitical power after the end of the Cold War.

In 2014, political scientist Walter Russell Mead published a prophetic article in *Foreign Affairs* titled "The Return of Geopolitics: The Revenge of Revisionist Powers". Mead's main thesis is that the unipolar world order based on US dominance, which has characterized the post-Cold War years, has come to an end, roughly since the outbreak of the financial crisis of 2007–2008. New revisionist powers, including China and Russia, uncomfortable with the US monopoly of power and armed with "revisionist" intentions, were about to challenge the established *status quo*. In particular, as has recently been openly stressed by *The Economist*, the challenge is aimed at the cultural complex of Western values ("China's Latest Attempt to Rally the World against Western Values. Xi Jinping Faults America for Any Clash of Civilisations", *The Economist*, April 27, 2023). With different degrees of assertiveness and power, both these autocracies have openly contested the existing hierarchy of power and the nexus between liberal democracy and prosperity. In different ways and measures, both challengers had found the process of global integration to be a unique driver supporting their geopolitical ambitions. While Russia had put itself forward as the main supplier of energy to Europe, China and a number of East Asian economies, globalization had transformed China into the workshop of the world, and endowed it with enough surpluses in the balance of trade to enable it to embark on an ambitious strategy of geoeconomic leadership on the Eurasian and African continents, and now, albeit tentatively, even in South America.

Globalization, to sum up, has provided revisionist powers with the most effective weapons to fight what Robert Blackwill and Jennifer Harris, two influential fellows of the US Council on Foreign Relations, have defined as "war by other means" in a book published in 2017, at the very start of Donald Trump's aggressive strategy aimed at limiting China's economic and political ascent to power.

As noted by one of the most acute analysts of the present status of world politics and economic affairs, former *Financial Times* chief economic commentator Martin Wolf ("Unsettling Precedents for Today's world", *Financial Times*, October 26, 2019) the present globalization process has recreated a very similar geopolitical situation to that in the decades preceding the Great War. The process of global integration following the Napoleonic Wars took place in a world dominated by empires, in a geopolitical framework of relative peace in Europe ensured by the first "Concert of Europe", based on a multipolar equilibrium with one hegemon leading power: Great Britain. This situation was destined to change with the unstoppable emergence of a "revisionist" great power in Europe that posed a challenge to the established *status quo*. The process of German unification (1866–1871) was the political outcome of the ascent of a geoeconomic protagonist, strengthened by the concomitant process of economic integration.

In geopolitical terms, considering the last 200 years, globalization sooner or later creates the conditions in which an emerging power challenges the *status quo* represented by an incumbent dominant power, as recently noted by another political scientist, Graham Allison, in his 2018 bestseller *Destined for War: Can America and China Escape Thucydides's Trap?*

1.4 Fourth reason: globalization and its futures

The process of global integration which has characterized the post-1989 decades has transformed the world's economy, introduced opportunities and perils for individuals and countries, promoted processes of social integration, and provoked cultural and political backlashes. It has set in motion powerful forces and reanimated powerful old ideas like cosmopolitanism, but has also reignited the reaction against its excesses, in the form of populist nationalisms. It has been a controversial process, whose dynamics have not always been easy to analyze and understand. What is beyond any doubt is that, as introduced above, after 20 years during which the process of global integration proceeded uncontested, also due to the strong political, institutional and ideological support of neoliberal ideologies, its endogenous contradictions began to present serious obstacles. Geopolitical assertiveness and social inequality have been eroding globalization from within, so what comes next?

In a "technical note" published as Harvard Business School teaching material in March 2022, business historians Valeria Giacomin and Geoffrey Jones stress the evident slowing, if not the actual decline, of the globalization process, and identify several causes of this, which include global terrorism, the 2008–2009 global financial crisis, the rise of populism and authoritarian regimes, and the geopolitical rivalry between the US and China. While it is possible to debate the real impact of these causes, the four possible alternative future scenarios they suggest for globalization are far more realistic.

A first, relatively optimistic, view sees the globalization process returning to normal via the contribution of technological progress, the resilience of global exchanges and the willingness of countries "blessed" by the process of global integration, with the only possible change introduced by the refocus of global trade on China.

A second possibility, perhaps when techno-nationalistic stances are brought into the framework, is a return to the interwar reality of isolated autarchic economies based on high levels of State intervention.

A more optimistic outlook envisages the birth of supra-regional aggregates in which integration does take place, but with a greatly reduced level of geographic range, probably around pivots such as the US, China, and perhaps the EU and India.

The fourth and much more unsettling scenario is that of growing assertiveness among the great powers, culminating in trade wars and attempts to secure control of strategic resources, which will lead to a rise in conflictual behavior, including the risk of a direct military clash, as notoriously happened with the outbreak of the Great War.

To assign a degree of probability to these multiple futures requires detailed knowledge of what globalization means, of the possible risks inherent in the deterioration, or downsizing of the process of integration which has driven global integration since 1989. In this sense, this book is "nostalgic" because it deals with what we do have and are about to lose – the globalization we may leave behind us – something that generations Z and Alpha (the cohorts born after 1989), who have grown up in conditions of permanent globalization, seem unable to comprehend.

As suggested earlier in this chapter, historians can compare different historical periods, and so they can propose possible future developments by looking at the ways similar dynamics have developed in the past. However, to do this, it is vital to have a much more detailed understanding of the process of global integration. For decades this process has constituted the framework for the action of politicians at domestic and international levels, of institutions of global cooperation, and, not least, of investors and companies building the sophisticated organizational structures that thrive in this integrated space.

1.5 This book

In order to achieve this objective, this book is divided into three main "blocks". The first section, including the present introduction and Chapter 2, is intended to "set the stage". In particular, a detailed historical narration in Chapter 2 provides a perspective on the dynamics characterizing the globalization of the "past", from the end of the Napoleonic Wars to the interwar period of the 20th century. This historical account is valuable for many reasons, including the extremely important fact that it has been a complete cycle, including the definitive collapse into a multi-decennial de-globalization process. To state this in a specific way, this is an instructive "relic of the past" and shows in detail which combination of forces can alter the globalization process to such an extent that within one or two generations it is rapidly transformed into a "slow-balization" trend or, even worse, into a retreat from global integration. Of course, there is a radical difference between causation and correlation, but the global war which followed underlines the closely intertwined relationship between the two phenomena.

Once the instructive story of 19th century global integration has been investigated, the rest of the book focuses on the extent of globalization in terms of its "size". The extent of globalization is mainly indicated via a series of different quantitative indicators, as shown in Chapter 3. Moreover, the existence of multiple globalizations in time and in the long term implies the impossibility of providing homogeneous data for comparing the distant past with the recent present. For instance, data on trade flows and tariffs have been systematically collected only for the two last globalization waves, and not for all the countries involved in global exchanges until the second half of the 19th century. Chapter 3, therefore, provides an overview of the different methods used by historians to assess the integration process for the specific historical phase under investigation.

Measurement of the globalization trends introduces investigation of their drivers. This book discusses technological, institutional and cultural drivers in a more general political and geopolitical framework. All operate simultaneously, although with different degrees of intensity over time and within the single cycle of globalization. In addition to directly influencing the intensity and "smoothness" of the process, these drivers also mutually impact on each other. In particular, if globalization trends are directly impacted by technological, institutional and cultural elements (as analyzed in Chapter 4), it is important to note how globalization itself impacts on political drivers, which can positively or negatively influence the other determinants of the process.

The "macro" impacts of globalization, particularly of the two most recent waves, have been widely investigated by economic historians. In what remains the most detailed and comprehensive attempt to examine the waves of trade globalization over 1,000 years (the second millennium),[1] economic historians Robert Findlay and Kevin O'Rourke provide a comprehensive assessment of the process of global integration from the so-called *Pax Mongolica* until the opening of the third millennium. In contrast, this book focuses on the "micro" aspect of the process, looking at the long-term evolution of international traders and multinational enterprises (Chapter 5). International business has naturally flourished in phases of globalization, evolving its organizational shape in a complex interaction with the macroeconomic environment. However, business historians have demonstrated that multinational companies have also been able to adapt their activities via appropriate strategies and techniques even during phases of slow-balization and de-globalization like that of the interwar years.

The importance of the political dimension in the globalization process, as emphasized in this book, has brought us to include an additional chapter (Chapter 6) which analyzes the internationalization of State-owned enterprises, a process which has accelerated during recent decades in both developing and developed economies. The emergence of these "State-owned multinationals" is a specific feature of the current globalization wave, but is also an effective demonstration of the complex political impacts of the globalization process itself. Governments increasingly recur to State-owned enterprises not only as instruments for regulating the domestic economy – for instance, in managing natural monopolies – but as a way to interact with the global economic framework in order to pursue both geopolitical and geoeconomic goals.

As emphasized at the start of this chapter, the present globalization wave, which began at the end of the Cold War, is now on the verge of an epochal turning point, the starting point of the multiple scenarios described above. The last chapter therefore focuses on the present situation of globalization by looking at the dynamics of the technological, institutional, cultural and political "drivers" mentioned above in order to reach a more effective evaluation of the multiple alternatives for the future.

1.6 Abstracting globalization

Before proceeding with the narrative, it is necessary to provide a generic definition of globalization that can be transversally applied to different historical phases. As Chapter 3 will show in detail, there are many definitions of globalization; despite the historical period of reference, these share some abstract traits. In abstract, the term "globalization" describes a process of rapid and extensive "integration". The extent of integration is "global", but "global" is a relative concept. Historians of globalization, for instance, include in this category processes of integration which are not exactly global in the sense that they do not extend to the entire globe, but do transcend the "local", regional and national dimensions. For instance, ancient and modern empires have created a process of integration inside their borders, even if not on a global scale. Historians of the Middle Ages and of the Renaissance use the term "globalization" when they describe the system of Atlantic Exchange between Europe, Africa and the Americas (see Chapter 3) or the commercial revolution of the Middle Ages, which linked areas previously completely independent of each other. A truly global and planetary process of globalization is definitely the one described in Chapter 2 of this book, followed by the present globalization, which is even more "planetary".

More importantly, such a process of integration is multidimensional. As this book will show in detail, it includes different types of integration processes: economic, cultural, institutional and also political.

In addition to being a multidimensional and dynamic process of integration, another recurrent feature of globalization is that the process is far from monotonic; on the contrary, it occurs in successive waves, consisting of different phases. A globalization wave may be represented as in Figure 1.2, where:

g is a generic measure of the intensity of exchanges as defined above

t is time

a is a phase where the rate of growth of exchanges is considerable and increases during every unit of time. This phase of "globalization" proper may be preceded by a phase of maturation of the conditions that allow globalization to definitively take off, and which may be defined as "re-globalization".

b is a phase in which there is a slowing down of the rate of growth of exchanges, unit of time by unit of time, until it slows to a level close to zero. This phase is "slow-balization".

c is the "de-globalization" phase, in which the intensity of exchanges decreases significantly.

Another detail emerging from historical research is that waves follow each other in the long term, normally lasting several decades. They are of course different in their dynamic evolution across space and time. What determines accelerations, slowdowns and declines in the shape of the wave are the "drivers" introduced above (see Chapter 4 for greater detail, consisting of technological progress, institutional arrangements, cultural attitudes, and other factors connected to politics, such as the climate of international relations among polities, the geopolitical structural balance and, not least, the nature of the domestic political system).

For instance, the last two centuries have been characterized by two long waves, which in turn consist of seven sub-periods:

   i) 1815–1850s: re-globalization
  ii) 1850s–1870s: globalization
 iii) 1870–1920s: slow-balization
 iv) 1920s–1950s: de-globalization
  v) 1950s–1990s: re-globalization
 vi) 1990s–2010s: globalization
vii) 2010s–present: slow-balization

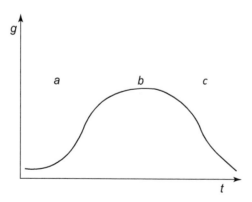

Figure 1.2 A globalization wave

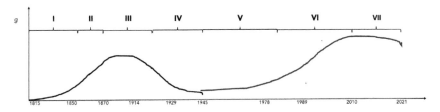

Figure 1.3 Globalization waves, 1815–2020

These can be visually represented as shown in Figure 1.3.

The same exercise can of course be repeated by including previous episodes of regional globalization or partial globalization, like the integration of Eurasian trading and cultural exchanges during the *Pax Mongolica*, or the subsequent phases of acceleration in exchanges among continental systems that characterized the post-Columbian centuries.

The rest of this book will be dedicated to in-depth analysis of the concept of globalization, its drivers and phases, also focusing on the entrepreneurs, traders and companies which were both agents and subjects of the powerful forces of global integration and disintegration.

Note

1 Robert Findlay and Kevin O'Rourke, *Power and Plenty: Trade, War and the World Economy in the Second Millennium*, Princeton University Press, 2007.

Chapter 2

The World of Yesterday

THE GLOBALIZATION THAT WAS (AND WHAT IT HAS TO TEACH US)

A S MANY READERS WILL REALIZE, THE title of this chapter paraphrases the title of the 1942 autobiographical novel *The World of Yesterday: Memories of a European* by Austrian writer Stefan Zweig (1942). In his memoirs, the author provides an effective and emotional glimpse of the world as it was before the First World War: The World of Yesterday.

The aim of this chapter is to guide the reader during through a phase in world history that was characterized by an intense process of "globalization", as defined in Chapter 1. Of course, Zweig's contemporaries did not use this term; they preferred the exotic and sophisticated-sounding *cosmopolitan*, a word of Greek origin, to indicate the borderless reality of cultural, scientific and economic exchanges that characterized the long phase in world history stretching from the end of the Napoleonic Wars to the deflagration of the First World War. The First World War brought this phase of global integration to a tragic end, transforming it into something that belongs to the past: a world "of yesterday".

For today's reader, keen to understand the dynamics of today's global integration and its foreseeable future, this journey is particularly important. The present globalization is not the first of its kind to occur in world history, although it does have its own characteristics and specific features. However, many of its basic features are also to be found in the past, and resonate even more loudly in the global integration of the "long" 19th century. More importantly, this previous globalization provides a very important indication about the possible future of the present global integration, showing what happens when the powerful forces that make it all work derail and disband, turning globalization into its opposite: fragmentation (see Chapter 7).

DOI: 10.4324/9780429490255-2

Nineteenth-century globalization had some specific attributes: for example, it was *borderless*, thanks to *technological progress*.

2.1 Global travelers

Macroscopic evidence of a borderless world is provided by the massive transfer of human beings, with intense travel taking place in an increasingly interconnected space.

Starting in the mid-1800s, mass migration accelerated across the globe, and an endless stream of migrants began to cross both land and sea, permanently or semi-permanently relocating to new destinations. It has been calculated that the second half of the 19th century saw no less than 60–70 million people migrate along long-distance routes across the Atlantic and Pacific Oceans, Siberia and Asia. Although religious and political considerations also played an important role in the decision to emigrate, migrants were mainly driven by the pressure of globalization itself. This was the case for Northern Italy's peasants, who were displaced by falling grain prices, a consequence of the steady fall in transportation costs, which enabled cheaper foodstuffs to flood the Italian market.

Thanks to new transport and communication technologies, and to an institutional framework that favored freedom of movement (see Chapter 4) distances steadily shrank, facilitating the often-painful movement of human beings in this densely interconnected world. Before it became a favorite subject for novels and dramatic movies, the *Titanic* was a transatlantic passenger ship. When it famously sank in 1912, its first-class passengers were the rich, influential and famous "happy few". However, a remarkable proportion of its over 2,200 passengers (most of whom died in the icy waters of the North Atlantic) were traveling in second, and above all third class. These were mainly migrants traveling in crowded conditions, some crossing the Atlantic for the first time, some sailing back to their new homeland after visiting their native countries.

However, the tragic end of the *Titanic* is not the only sad and touching outcome of this globalized world. The archives of Ellis Island record every immigrant who entered the US from 1892, and preserve touching memories of a tumultuous flow of human beings. At its peak of activity, between 1900 and 1914, approximately 5–10,000 people passed through the gates of the immigration processing center every single day.

Europeans sailed even to the most remote regions of the globe, like Australia, New Zealand and Siberia. Asians also moved, and one example of this is the massive wave of Chinese migration to the Americas during the last decades of the 19th century.

Needless to say, these diasporas often caused disruption to local societies and labor markets, giving rise to harsh anti-immigration movements.

However, migrants in search of a better living (or simply aiming to survive) were not the only people moving around in this borderless space. Together with poverty-stricken migrants, the *Titanic* also transported another social group of people traveling for pleasure. These tourists moved alone or bought places on the first organized trips, like those offered by the Thomas Cook travel agency. Founded in 1841 by a British entrepreneur, in the 1850s it began to regularly sell organized trips to Continental Europe (including the Swiss Alps and Italy) and Africa. In the late 1860s, Cook's began taking British tourists across the Atlantic to the US, and from 1872 the world's most important travel agency offered its customers a "World Tour Package". Cook's clients traveled westward, crossing the Atlantic to New York, taking the train to San Francisco, sailing to Japan, China, Singapore and India, and then through the Suez Canal into the Mediterranean and the Middle East, finally arriving back in Europe after more than seven months.

At this time, vast regions of the globe were still unknown to Europeans and attracted the most audacious and extreme form of tourism: exploration. Norwegian Roald Amundsen was the first to successfully traverse the North-west Passage between 1903 and 1906, sailing from Greenland to Alaska. In the mean time, Africa was a target for Victorian explorers like the legendary David Livingstone, while geographers and surveyors tirelessly explored the most remote corners of Central Asia, mapping rivers and Himalayan peaks alike.

Others again traveled not for necessity, pleasure or glory, but because they saw travel as the best way to acquire knowledge. "Educational travel" was already a standard practice of the European aristocracy in the 18th century. The 19th century made these travels less poetic and more "practice-oriented". Promising students traveled to acquire new ideas and entrepreneurial opportunities, as in the case of a brilliant graduate of the Milan Polytechnic, Giovanni Battista Pirelli. Before founding an innovative business in the *caoutchouc* industry in 1872, Pirelli spent several months roaming around Europe in search of "a new industry", as he said.

While Pirelli was traveling alone in Europe, others were doing the same, but in a much more organized way. Between 1871 and 1873 a Japanese "study mission" of around 100 people, including prominent government officials and brilliant students, travelled from Yokohama to the US. The "Iwakura Mission", known by the name of its leader, aimed to visit various countries around the world in order to accelerate the process of institutional modernization in post-Meiji Restoration Japan (Westney, 1987).

2.2 Global places

The world across which this variegated kaleidoscope of travelers moved back and forth was borderless and interconnected. However, borders did actually exist, even if they were permeable. In the global world of the 19th century, the standard political unit was the empire: either a formal empire or, as in the case of the US, a multi-state aggregation of continental size. It has been calculated that roughly two-thirds of the world's population lived under an empire during the second half of the 19th century. Empires were large and sometimes immense entities, both the continental land empires like the Ottoman, Russian, Austro-Hungarian and Chinese empires, and also the "empires by sea" like the British and French empires, which included distant overseas territories. At the same time, there were also some relatively minor empires, like the Dutch and the German empires in remote areas of Southeast Asia and the Western Pacific.

Many, if not all, of the migration flows described above took place within the borders of empires – for instance, the colonization of Siberia. Empires persistently and aggressively expanded their dominion, either via direct confrontation with each other, as in the case of the "Great Game" played out between Britain and Russia in Central Asia, or via international agreements. Between 1884 and 1885, the representatives of the European, US and Ottoman governments gathered in Berlin to effect the peaceful partition of an entire continent: Africa. The so-called Congo Conference settled, or rather regulated, what has been defined as a "scramble": the rush to acquire territories and colonies in Africa. From then on, the continent was an essential component of the World of Yesterday, at least as a source of natural resources and destination of colonial settlements.

Empires were complex and sophisticated bodies, with very different impacts on their subject populations; these were not only negative, but frequently also positive impacts such as political and cultural integration. To a large extent, the empires contributed to the reduction of many information asymmetries and transaction costs, at least for a part of their populations, as any British citizen traveling within the British Empire could confirm.

At the other extreme of the dimensional spectrum in this increasingly connected and interlinked world, some international "hubs" emerged in the form of cities that were simultaneously the destination and the starting point of the human (but not exclusively) flows characterizing the global world. It was not only a matter of their size, which in almost all cases was quite remarkable, but it was also a case of strategic positioning in the flows of globalization, and of specialization in trade-related services.

Many – but not all – of these "global cities" were port cities, since the main physical flows of trade and migrants traveled via sea, and the main overland transportation routes converged on these ports. From San Francisco to New York, Singapore, Calcutta, Cape Town, Hong Kong, Canton, Shanghai and Yokohama (a small Japanese fishing village designated an open port for foreign trade in 1859), all these cities became lively hubs during the second half of the 19th century as global flows converged and traversed them, like the sand in an hourglass. All shared some characteristics that are still common features of global cities today: apart from being hubs of international trade and finance, they hosted a cosmopolitan melting-pot of different entrepreneurial populations and were centers of lively innovation; despite their independence, they were also key components in their respective home countries' geopolitical positioning.

This global world was, therefore, intensely traveled, explored, networked and migrated. Necessity, sport, leisure, risk or simply the thirst for knowledge led millions of human beings to remote destinations, mixing them in an endless process of integration. Of course, the new migrants tended to cluster in communities defined by their common origin, language or religious faith, like Boston's Catholic community of Italians and Irish in the city's North End and East areas, and the Little Italy and Chinatown quarters in all the rapidly expanding US towns and cities. However, the sense of a borderless global community was a common intellectual trait of a large section of the intellectual bourgeoisie.

2.3 Global cosmopolitanism

Tokens and memorials of the World of Yesterday are still visible today, like the Eiffel Tower in Paris. The Champ de Mars where the Tower stands was the most crowded area of an already crowded city at the start of the last century of the second millennium and was the venue of the 1900 Paris *Exposition Universelle*. The *Exposition* remained open from April to November and was an iconic celebration of the world's new global identity forged during the decades following the Napoleonic Wars.

During the seven months of the *Exposition*, almost 50 million visitors (many of whom had traveled with Thomas Cook) crowded into the fair's pavilions, whose contents allowed them to "travel" the world. As they walked the streets of the Champ de Mars, visitors could not help seeing the Eiffel Tower, but another wonderful attraction was also the center of attention: the giant Globe Céleste, a telling symbol of an increasingly pervasive cosmopolitan and globalized culture.

Everything pointed towards the fascinating idea of cosmopolitanism in a borderless world. At the same time as its international fair, Paris was also the celebrated venue of the second edition of the modern version of the Olympic Games, a sporting event that was essentially a celebration of universalism.

A consequence of this incessant movement of people, and another distinctive feature (albeit far less "miserable" than others) of this 19th century globalization, was a pervasive *cosmopolitan* culture. Cosmopolitanism here means being firmly rooted in the familiar home setting, in the basic unit of the family, the ethnic community, the neighborhood and the nation, and at the same time being able to focus on what was far from the local setting, on a community of human beings that existed above and beyond any national identity.

Nineteenth-century cosmopolitan culture coexisted with nationalist movements for a long time, at least until the trenches of the First World War opened their muddy jaws. It would be easy to label cosmopolitanism as a distinctive cultural trait of the elites. It was certainly the pervasive atmosphere in the ethnic and intellectual melting pots of Europe's cosmopolitan cities like Vienna. However, a Sicilian *picciotto* waiting in the long lines at Ellis Island could not avoid the impression of being a member of the Sicilian community in New York, but also an Italian (if emigrating after Italian Unification in 1861) and one of the many thousands passing through US immigration controls, one of a global community of migrants, who were ultimately not so radically different from each other apart from their distinctive styles of dress.

2.4 Global capital

The phase that lasted from the end of Napoleonic Wars until the First World War was marked by a steady rise in the level of world economic integration, accompanied by an increasing openness of trade, which is clearly shown by the growth of capital mobility and cross-border investments. Chapter 4 will focus in depth on these dynamics.

However, trade flows are just one component of this openness. According to Findlay and O'Rourke (2007), average annual growth in the volume of international trade stood at 3.85 percent throughout the 19th century, in contrast with a mere 1 percent during the previous three centuries. A key driver in this dynamic was the progressive removal of the existing trade barriers: considering the Western developed countries, in the second half of the 19th century the average openness ratio (of imports to GDP) rose constantly, while the protection ratio (custom revenues on total imports) fell to just half the level it had been before 1850.

In some cases, the change in approach was remarkable. For example, the UK protection ratio stood at approximately 0.5 at the beginning of the century, but on the eve of the First World War this had dropped to just 0.05. Since the commercial revolution of the Middle Ages, international trade was not a novelty, but the "new" element was its apparently unstoppable and outstanding growth in volume, speed and above all *global* reach, coupled with a drop in inflation.

Nowadays, one of the most popular visitor destinations in Shanghai is the city's old riverside mercantile area known as the Bund. The crowds of tourists wandering its streets are perhaps too busy taking selfies and photos of Pudong's financial center and its skyscrapers to look over at the opposite side of the street, lined with beautifully restored old buildings. Brick and stone facades bear witness to Shanghai's "colonial" past, when foreign companies rushed to establish the headquarters of their subsidiaries right there in the heart of the city.

Now covered in red flags, one of the area's most beautiful buildings is worth visiting. Today it is a branch of the Bank of China, but it was built between 1921 and 1923 as the Shanghai headquarters of the Hong Kong and Shanghai Banking Corporation (HSBC). The bank was founded in Hong Kong and Shanghai in 1865 by Scottish entrepreneur and banker Thomas Sutherland in order to finance trade (including the opium trade) in China and Southeast Asia. The building's lavish architecture features multi-colored marble and its dome is decorated with allegorical portraits of the world's largest cities, those that were already, or were quickly becoming, the most important financial centers: global cities, the capitals of capital (Cassis, 2006).

Starting from the second half of the 19th century, financial capital became probably the most "globalized" input in the world. Investments circulated freely, and profits were repatriated or reinvested without friction or obstacles. Capital was invested everywhere in state and private bonds and other securities, including shares in business ventures even in remote areas of the globe. Western enterprises opened subsidiaries everywhere that market opportunities made it desirable and reasonable to do so. The index of overall capital mobility rose steadily between 1850 and 1914 to a level reached again only at the beginning of the new millennium.

Of course, this kind of revolution in trade and finance was enabled by the new information and communication technologies; these rapidly eliminated information asymmetries, promoted price convergence, and allowed investors to have all the information they needed quickly and easily. However, a key contribution to this economic globalization also came from institutional arrangements that contained an element of uncertainty. The most remarkable example of this institutional support to the first global economy is probably the establishment of the Gold Standard, an international agreement that began in the 1870s and linked the value of a currency to the quantity of a country's gold reserves, given that gold was freely transferable between countries. On the positive side, the Gold Standard led to relatively low inflation, and above all, to a relatively stable system of exchange rates, so that the overall effect on international trade and finance flows was positive.

2.5 Global imperialism

It was impossible to avoid being contaminated by "globalization", particularly in a world whose the standard political unit was "the empire". As supranational entities, there is no doubt that empires allowed smoother and frictionless organization of trade within and beyond their vast borders. Thanks to the presence of skilled dynasties of merchants and traders (Jones, 2000), empires were home to sophisticated structures of exchange, as exemplified by the tripartite value chain based on poppy cultivation in the Indian subcontinent. This was coordinated by British merchants, with products marketed as painkilling pharmaceuticals in Western Europe and as narcotics (opium) in China.

Some ancient and glorious empires were kept alive because of their strategic control over vital communication routes, as in the case of the Ottoman Empire, which included the Dardanelles and the Suez Canal. Others were subjugated to serve the international global trade, as in the case of China.

However, it was not only empires that came under the unavoidable pressure of globalization. Several countries were obliged to radically transform the structure of their own economic systems in order to face competitive challenges from other areas of the world that were now entering the realm of international trade for the first time, thanks to the communication revolution. This was particularly the case for countries in search of a new identity and a favorable position in the world's power hierarchy. One of these was Italy, which experienced a profound reorientation of its national economy from the 1870s, as the emphasis shifted from agriculture to an intense process of industrialization; this was triggered by the competitive challenge of low-cost foodstuffs and agricultural products that flooded into Europe from the Russian Empire and the Americas as an unavoidable effect of the compression of time and space.

In other cases, globalization literally compelled countries, whether willing or not, to undertake a full restructuring process in order to cope with the new world order.

It is ironic that one of the last countries to allow whale hunting today is Japan (together with Norway). This may be the price whales are still paying for their role in forcing Japan to abandon two centuries of voluntary isolation from the rest of the world. This isolationist policy, known as *sakoku* (see Chapter 3) aimed to preserve Japanese independence, sovereignty and autonomy. However, after 200 years, whales made this isolation simply obsolete. In fact, globalization came knocking at Japan's door in November 1853, when US Navy Commodore Matthew Perry led four "black ships" into Edo (now Tokyo) Bay. His purpose was to deliver a letter from US president Millard Fillmore to the Japanese Emperor, whose subjects considered him a divinity. The tone of the missive was formally respectful, but in reality, the message was openly assertive, and whales were most definitely a driving force.

> I have directed Commodore Perry to mention another thing to your imperial majesty. Many of our ships pass every year from California to China; *and great numbers of our people pursue the whale fishery near the shores of Japan. It sometimes happens, in stormy weather, that one of our ships is wrecked on your imperial majesty's shores.* In all such cases we ask, and expect, that our unfortunate people should be treated with kindness, and that their property should be protected, till we can send a vessel and bring them away. (emphasis added)
>
> (Masahiro et al., 1853)

Whale hunting was a key industry in the second half of the 19th century, one of the largest in the US. In a world of darkness, whales provided light: their strong-smelling blubber oil was the main combustible used for lighting as well as for lubricating delicate mechanisms like clocks. Whale bones were also a key component in women's clothing. As a result, whale-hunting became one of the world's most profitable industries for a number of decades. In the mid-19th century around 900 whaling ships (nearly four out of five were registered in the US) sailed the oceans, intent on killing their own Moby Dick, like the captain in Herman Melville's 1851 masterpiece of the same name.

Unfortunately for Japan and for its desire to isolate from the rest of the world, it now became a geopolitical necessity for the country to enter the new global economy. Whales were abundant in the Pacific, and Japan was also seen in the US as the perfect doorway to China and South-East Asia. Under the urgent pressure of globalization and driven to preserve its independence, Japan was compelled to develop a new outlook.

The most progressive elites now seized power. The emperor became the symbol of modern Japan, replacing the old military dictatorship that had actually governed the country for the past two centuries. The country voluntarily and eagerly Westernized, importing from Europe and the US the most efficient and valuable ingredients of the recipe for development: institutions.

Keen to modernize at any cost, the Japanese government tapped Western countries to copy and adapt the most organized armies (France and Germany), the most efficient postal service and navy (Great Britain), the best primary education systems (France and the US) and many other examples of progress, thus creating the basis for the consolidation and astonishing success of the country in the first half of the 20th century (Westney, 1987).

No differently from Japan, remote regions across the globe were flung into the global economy, which transformed their productive specializations, and at times even their "physical" structures. Intensive plantations of non-native staple products profoundly altered the landscape of entire countries, as in the case of rubber tree and palm oil plantations in South-East Asia or poppy growing in the north-western regions of the Indian subcontinent.

In short, economic globalization altered certain equilibria that had remained unchanged for centuries, posing new challenges to the world's geopolitical order and to the existent power hierarchies among nations.

2.6 Global technology

The World of Yesterday was technological. French novelist Jules Verne (1828–1905) is a significant example of how the technological progress of the 19th century impacted, for instance, on fictional writing. In almost all his best-known books, technological innovations and modern artifacts play a key role and are always at center stage. In Verne's stories, fabulous machines are made possible by new technologies, and what had been pure fantasy becomes real and possible. His characters were able to travel under the sea, to the depths of the Earth, and in space. Above all, new technologies shrank distances, making it possible to travel much faster than before and in a much more organized and efficient way.

The essence of Verne's message, in a sense, is "traveling", but this "traveling" is so profoundly transformed by technology that modern travelers are totally different from their predecessors. The symbol of all this is Phileas Fogg, the hero of Verne's worldwide bestseller, *Around the World in Eighty Days*, which was published for the first time in 1873. This precise, brilliant and wealthy English gentleman, who wagered that he could travel around the world in under 80 days, was actually modeled on a real character, the American entrepreneur, financier and adventurer George Francis Train. Also real were those who in the wake of the novel's success attempted to repeat Fogg's fictional achievement. One was the American journalist Nellie Bly, who in 1889 made a successful journey around the world in just 72 days.

Unlike other famous characters created by Verne, including cosmonaut Michel Ardan and submariner Captain Nemo, Phileas Fogg did not travel in the future. Fogg achieved his extraordinary *tour de force* simply by making creative use of the opportunities offered by the "new" means of transportation and communication. In his counter-clockwise tour of the world, Fogg used each available cutting-edge technology: steamships enabling safe and rigorously punctual travel, fast trains and even hot-air balloons. The recently opened Suez Canal allowed Fogg to avoid the time-consuming route around the Horn of Africa. He communicated by telegraph and received constant news updates from the newspapers that he found almost everywhere he went.

Fogg was truly cosmopolitan and felt at home everywhere in the world. He journeyed in safety, barely showing his passport thanks to the worldwide acceptance of the British sterling; after all, he was an Englishman, and a large part of his trip involved travel in British colonies and protectorates (India and Hong Kong), British informal dominions (China), recently Westernized countries (Japan), and former British colonies (the US). He hardly ever bothered to use a different language from his own. With all his limits and negative traits, including his deep and persistent racism, Fogg symbolizes a world that had been radically transformed during the course of the 19th century by new technology that made it for the first time truly global.

The technologies of the First and Second Industrial Revolutions, like the steam engine, mechanics, steel and electricity, became widespread and made globalization possible by enabling one of the essential features of each globalization: "time-space compression". Technology really revolutionized transportation and profoundly affected how a considerable section of society perceived the world and its geography. This revolution was itself the logical consequence of widespread application of the most important general-purpose technologies of the industrial revolutions: steam power and electricity were used to enhance travel by land and sea, and to improve communications.

Starting from the early 1830s, railroads quickly spread all over Europe, Asia, North and South America, and international connections swiftly followed. In the second half of the century, there were even greater impacts from the design and completion of ambitious projects to connect remote regions to transport and communications networks. On his world tour, Phileas Fogg leaves San Francisco by train, traveling eastwards to New York, setting out on a trip which he estimated would take him a week, but which had required six months before completion of the Pacific Railroad in 1869. Another inter-continental connector was the Trans-Siberian railroad linking Moscow to Vladivostok; built between 1891 and 1916, it was completed only a few months before the Bolshevik Revolution of 1917. Rail travel had improved so much that by the first decades of the 20th century, apart from gauge differences, it was possible to travel on an almost unbroken railroad network stretching from Europe to China, another country that had embarked on a massive railroad-building project, using what was mainly foreign capital.

Similar connections involved the oceans, with long-distance steamship lines linking the continents. In late August 1833, just a couple of years after the first railroad was inaugurated in the UK, the SS *Royal William* docked at the British port of Gravesend in Kent after a smooth voyage of several weeks from Pictou, Nova Scotia. This apparently unexceptional event actually marked an important turning point in history because the *Royal William* had crossed the Atlantic using only steam power, her sails remaining idle unless boiler maintenance was necessary.

Starting in the early 1840s, steamships began crossing the Atlantic and other seas regularly. There was nothing novel about international shipping and sea travel, but what was new here was the way technology impacted on sea travel in terms of speed and reliability. The revolutionary impact of railroads and steamers was not only about the overall duration of journeys, particularly over land; it was above all about *punctuality*. "On time" is a recurrent sentence in time-obsessed Phileas Fogg's journey around the globe, and steamers and trains now made possible what in the past had been impossible. Travelers were almost completely freed from the unpredictable impacts of weather conditions, and other wondrous advances would soon become possible.

Thanks to the SS *Great Eastern*, one of the wonders of the British Navy, it was possible to complete one of the most ambitious and legendary projects of the 19th century: a telegraph cable stretching across the Atlantic was completed in 1866. The steamer was carrying in her hull what was one of the key components of globalization: a cable. For the first time in history this would connect continents and enable direct communication.

Undersea cables were the next stage of another major innovation at the national and continental levels. The overland telegraph line connecting the East and West Coasts of the US was completed in October 1861. Its inauguration led to the immediate closure of the legendary Pony Express Service, unable to compete with a service that could deliver messages in just a few minutes or seconds instead of the ten days needed for a letter to cross the Great Plains and Rocky Mountains. The same was happening everywhere in the world, where dense "telegraph roads" spread across nations and continents to create an intense web of communications linking all regions of the globe.

Daily newspapers and magazines made news wired around the world readily available to all and at an affordable price, as they became progressively cheaper. The rotary printing press revolutionized the production of dailies in an astonishingly short span of time. In the 1840s, when the first prototypes of rotaries were introduced, printing speed surged to 4,000 pages an hour. In the 1850s, this doubled. Ten years later in the 1860s, the adoption of continuous paper rolls pushed capacity to 12,000 pages. Newspaper and information costs plummeted, with the result that daily newspaper circulation per household multiplied. Papers were often delivered to the house by increasingly efficient postal services, both national and international. Here is another component of the general revolution in information, communications and transportation that stood at the heart of the "first global world".

2.7 Global commons

> To Richard Cobden. Esq., M.P., London – *Cairo, December 3, 1854*. As the friend of peace, and of the Anglo-French alliance, I am going to tell you some news which will aid in realising the words, *Aperire Terram gentibus* ....
>
> (De Lesseps, 1876)

When he wrote this letter to the influential British statesman, Frenchman Ferdinand Marie de Lesseps was already in his late forties. He had just left a promising career as a high-ranking diplomat, a career which had taken him across Europe and the Mediterranean, to North Africa and the Middle East, which were all areas he had come to know well. He left a brilliant professional career to commit to a project that he considered a mission and much more than a business opportunity – a mission that also aimed to bring about peaceful coexistence among nations through their commitment to a "common good": the construction of a waterway, a connection. The Suez Canal, linking the Mediterranean to the Indian Ocean, was successfully completed in 1869.

In De Lesseps' perspective, "*aperire terram gentibus*", or "making the world accessible to everyone", was an essential component of a *Weltanschauung* shared by many intellectuals and statesmen of the time. It was the idea of global citizenship as a distinctive feature of the "modern" world, a natural consequence of the growing global openness and inter-connections: in a word, it was "cosmopolitanism". Cosmopolitan by nature and education, De Lesseps was committed to cutting down distances, and even in his seventies he was ready to travel to the US to persuade the country's leadership to commit to the creation of another global "shortcut": the Panama Canal.

2.8 Global imbalances

The first global world also had a number of dark sides, which are much more evident to us than they generally were to its contemporaries. Empires were, as stressed above, one of the basic building blocks of this global world. They were, however, a double-edged sword, agents both of inclusion but also of oppression. During the first globalization, empires were engaged in persistent and aggressive expansion of their dominion. This involved direct confrontation with each other, as in Central Asia during the "Great Game" between the Russian and the British empires, and it also involved international agreements that characterized the "Concert(s) of Europe", the informal agreements that ensured peace in Europe after the Napoleonic Wars and fostered the European partition of the world.

Between 1884 and 1885, for instance, the representatives of the European, US and Ottoman governments gathered in Berlin to peacefully divide up an entire continent between them: Africa. Well before the Berlin Conference, and following the Opium Wars, China had been carved up into spheres of influence of the foreign (European and Japanese) empires. This kind of domination was so taken for granted that when the US was expanding its sphere of influence in the Pacific and in the Caribbean at the end of the 19th century, it felt the need to assert its influence by issuing an "open note" to the other powers in order to reaffirm its trade rights in China.

The World of Yesterday was undoubtedly "Western". This was the logical consequence of what historians have called the "Great Divergence", a process of technological development, military build-up and rapid economic growth that began even before the First Industrial Revolution, underpinning the political supremacy of the West over the "rest".

In short, the empires embodied a profound contradiction. On the one hand, they were powerful symbols of globalization, in some way encompassing nationalities, and in some cases, for instance Austria-Hungary, they were able to embody the idea of cosmopolitanism in a concrete way, melting different nationalities together in the crucibles of their open and multicultural cities brimming with creativity. For instance, at the turn of the 20th century, Vienna's population of 2 million made it the sixth largest metropolis in the world, populated by Germans, Slovaks, Czechs, Slovenians, Poles, Italians and other "communities", including its pervasive Jewish community, who all contributed to the capital's cultural and intellectual creativity in arts and sciences.

At the same time, however, the empires frustrated the nationalistic aspirations of their subject peoples, their search for independence, autonomy and self-determination. In the case of overseas colonies, the empires explicitly created social hierarchies, division and distance between the colonizers and the colonized; this was a distance that could hardly ever be bridged. Imperial rule was frequently based on military occupation, terror and violence, making independence and freedom into even more compelling desires and political goals, as shown by the tragic destiny of the Belgian Congo. Above all, imperialism went hand-in-hand with another characteristic of the World of Yesterday, the spread of inequality.

Inequality was another global feature of the first global world. According to data published by the economists Thomas Piketty and Emmanuel Saez (2014), in the decades between 1870 and the First World War, the share of total wealth in the hands of the top 10 percent of the population grew constantly both in Europe and the US. Although little data is available about the rest, there is no reason to think that the most industrialized countries had significantly higher inequality levels than the peripheral countries. In 1910, the richest 10 percent of the population in Europe possessed 90 percent of the total wealth, and this is particularly striking given the almost total absence of welfare and redistribution programs. The enrichment of the "happy few" was clearly due to the transformations of the Second Industrial Revolution, and to the global economy.

Together with inequality, populism soon emerged as an ideology that ultimately supported the masses against the elites. This was a generic concept, which both right-wing and left-wing political movements could easily adapt to their own purposes, as quickly happened in the new Europe that emerged from devastation of the First World War.

2.9 Globalization and its discontents

August 3, 1914 is a symbolic date, one of the mere accidents of the unintended irony of history. In the short span of a few hours, two events occurred at opposite sides of the world, completely independent of each other. Yet they were in a certain way symbolically connected. The first event took place in a remote region of Central America when the passenger and cargo steamship *Cristobal* first traveled the Panama Canal, just before the Canal's official inauguration several weeks later. The Panama Canal had a long and troubled history; its construction took five years, starting in 1909 after a US-sponsored revolution in 1903 had essentially separated the Panama territories from Colombia. The work on the Canal was accelerated by the geopolitical expansion of the US into the Caribbean and Pacific, which began at the end of the 19th century with the Spanish-American War (1898), and also by the need to provide warships with a rapid passage between the two oceans. In some ways, the Panama Canal can be seen as the iconic high point of the first globalization. Its completion made it possible to circumnavigate the globe avoiding the long and dangerous routes used in the past, as in the case of the Magellan-Elcano expedition at the beginning of the 16th century.

However, an event in Europe on August 3 of that year symbolically brought the first globalization to an abrupt end. On the very same day, Germany declared war on France, and this triggered the devastation of the first great global conflict. As Stefan Zweig sadly commented in the first paragraphs of *The World of Yesterday*, the world he had known was like "a hollow clay pot breaking into a thousand pieces".

The First World War annihilated approximately 17 million lives and permanently damaged those of other 20 million. To make the tragedy even worse, in less than five years it brought an abrupt end to a global world that had developed over the last 60 years, during the period Zweig called "the Golden Age of Security". It crushed the institutions that had made the world open, and turned the technologies of transportation, communication and production into machines used for the mass killing of human beings.

As publishers know very well, understanding the origins of the First World War is one of the favorite playgrounds of historians, in a desperate attempt to find a rationale in something that surpasses all rationality. Whatever its origin and determinants, the implosion of the World of Yesterday was closely connected to the centripetal force of globalization and with the various forms of discontent it created.

The first global economy brought awareness of the evils of global markets, as felt by the masses. All over Europe, peasants learned about the ruthless laws of international trade, supported by the revolution in information and communications, and many were faced with the stark choice between living a life of hardship and poverty or joining the planetary migration. As stressed above, these large-scale migrations created discontent both in the migrant population and in those countries where the local population felt "invaded" by vast numbers of new migrants.

Secondly, globalization was closely linked to imperialism. After the partition of Africa during the Berlin Conference, little else remained to be colonized and subjugated. At the same time, the race for countries to expand their geopolitical sphere of influence proceeded; while some of the "old" empires were growing weaker, like the Ottoman empire, others in Europe and Asia were becoming increasingly aggressive. Cosmopolitanism, peace, international flows and chains, and globalization were all concepts that constituted serious obstacles and limits for those who gave precedence to national interests over all other considerations:

> Today, indeed, we live in a time which points with special satisfaction to the proud height of its culture, which is only too willing to boast of its international cosmopolitanism, and flatters itself with visionary dreams of the possibility of an everlasting peace throughout the world. This view of life is un-German and does not suit us. The German who loves his people, who believes

in the greatness and the future of our homeland, and who is unwilling to see its position diminished, dares not close his eyes in the indulgence of dreams such as these, he dares not allow himself to be lulled into indolent sleep by the lullabies of peace sung by the Utopians.

These words were written in 1913 by Crown Prince Wilhelm of Germany, son of Kaiser Wilhelm II, in a book entitled *Germany in Arms*, which is considered as a manifesto of the arms race that characterized the early 20th century. Wilhelm was adamant in stressing that the evil of globalization was that it needed peace to prosper, while peace and prosperity were undermining the spirit of the nation:

The old ideals, even the position and the honor of the nation, may be sympathetically affected; for peace, peace at any price, is necessary for the undisturbed acquisition of money.

Globalization also stimulated nationalistic sentiments in other ways. As anticipated above, the process of international economic integration had a devastating impact on China. Two Opium Wars and a series of unequal treaties granting special rights and privileges to foreign powers had transformed what had once been the world's proudest empire into a semi-colony. This permanent state of humiliation created a pervasive hostility towards foreigners, culminating in the 1899 Boxer Rebellion, which was quickly and harshly suppressed by the Allied Intervention Army of nine countries: Britain, the US, Australia, India, Germany, France, Austria-Hungary, Italy and Japan. Except for Italy, these were all empires or colonies of an empire.

The foreign occupation of China was followed by the fall of the Qing Dynasty in 1912 and by a devastating civil war. These events were so traumatic for China that it is not difficult to see in this painful phase of its history the origins of Chinese isolation under Communism before 1978, or of its cautious approach to international relations in the present.

In other cases, the inescapable pressure of the global economy led to quite different outcomes. When Tsar Alexander II abolished serfdom with the Emancipation Act of 1861, it was clear that the world's largest empire needed a vast number of reforms. The Crimean War in the 1850s had ended in another defeat for Russia by an allied intervention force, this time consisting of troops from France, the Ottoman Empire, Britain and the Kingdom of Sardinia. This clearly demonstrated Russia's need for modernization, and a necessary component of this was industrialization. The process accelerated in the 1870s when the government stimulated the construction of railroads, including the

Trans-Siberian (see above). Foreign investments followed; for example, the famous sewing-machine producer, Singer, opened a factory in Podolsk near Moscow in 1900. The expansion of industrial centers in the major Russian cities resulted in a rapid urbanization process. However, this was accompanied by a deterioration in the living conditions of urban workers, which paved the way for the waves of unrest that began in 1905 and culminated in the seizure of power by the Bolsheviks in 1917. Almost overnight, the Russian Revolution subtracted an important region of the world from the international economy for over 70 years.

Unable or unwilling to redistribute the gains of integration, prosperity and peace, the Age of Security killed its pupils: economic integration, cosmopolitanism, peace, cooperation and the possibility of travel without barriers. It left the world stage open to new actors: nationalisms, conflicts, dictatorships, closure and autarky, and, eventually, to another global war.

2.10 Conclusion

The story narrated in this chapter is the story of the globalization wave which originated after the tumultuous phase of the Napoleonic Wars, developed throughout the 19th century, peaked in the first decade of the 20th century, and abruptly ended in the years of the First World War and the "dark valley" of the two interwar decades. It is important to listen to this story because it teaches that globalization is not at all a monotonic process. On the contrary, it takes the form of a wave: it begins, accelerates, peaks and ends.

This story also has plenty to tell us about the determinants of globalization: about the role of technology, institutions, and culture, but also about the political micro- and macro-structures and the geopolitical framework which facilitate the overall process of integration.

There is also another important lesson to draw from the globalization wave preceding the present one: the dynamics described in this chapter were not frictionless in terms of their social impact. The economic globalization that followed the space-shrinking generated by the information and communication technology revolution was extremely positive in terms of offering increased business opportunities for companies, entrepreneurs, and even for marginal societies. However, it had a dramatic effect on other social groups, who saw the progressive loss of their economic security and their welfare, and who were ultimately forced to emigrate from their homelands in order to make a decent living elsewhere.

Globalization and trade had other medium-term impacts, for instance in terms of the geopolitical situation. The multipolar balance of power after the Napoleonic Wars was based upon the hegemonic leadership of Great Britain and on the multiple concerts of the European powers, but then this order was increasingly challenged by an emerging power, Germany, whose growing economic and military ambitions were fueled by its increasing leadership in the globalized economic space.

Rising inequality, growing imbalances and the rise of a challenger in the center of Europe triggered a powerful threat that ultimately imploded into a conflict like none before, which killed and buried the World of Yesterday.

As the rest of this book will show, many of the components of the global dynamics described in this chapter have returned in substance, if not in the same form, during the current process of world integration. Technology, institutions, cultural characteristics, their impacts on society, on interactions among states and on power ambitions have returned, as have the interactions among their variables. After a long process during which globalization has developed as an inescapable force, the world now stands at what has been defined as a "global *Zeitenwende*" (see Chapter 1). This is characterized by a slowing of all the indicators of economic, social and political interconnections, and old and new methods of assertiveness seem to prevail over a sense of international cooperation.

With this book, we hope at least to help the new generation to become aware of the perils and consequences implied by the descent into another "Dark Valley".

References

Youssef Cassis, *Capitals of Capital: A History of International Financial Centres, 1780–2005*. Cambridge: Cambridge University Press, 2006.

Robert Findlay and Kevin O'Rourke, *Power and Plenty: Trade, War and the World Economy in the Second Millennium*. Princeton: Princeton University Press, 2007.

Geoffrey Jones, *Merchants to Multinationals: British Trading Companies in the 19th and 20th Centuries*. Oxford: Oxford University Press, 2000.

De Lesseps Ferdinand Marie, *The Suez Canal, Letters and documents descriptive of its rise and progress in 1854–1856*, London: Henry King and Co., p. 36. 1876.

Abe Masahiro, Associated Name, Millard Fillmore, and Matthew Calbraith Perry. *Gasshūkoku Shokan Wage*. [Place of publication not identified: Publisher not identified, 1853] Pdf. Retrieved from the Library of Congress, <www.loc.gov/item/2021667464/>.

Thomas Piketty and Emmanuel Saez, "Inequality in the long run", *Science*, 344(6186), 2014: 838–843.

Eleanor Westney, *Imitation and Innovation: The Transfer of Western Organizational Patterns to Meiji Japan*. Cambridge: Harvard University Press, 1987.

Stefan Zweig, *The World of Yesterday: Memories of a European*, New York: Viking Press, 1943.

Chapter 3

Measuring globalization

3.1 Measuring globalization: relevance and challenges

Globalization's wave-like trend means that in order to understand its dynamics, it is crucial to be able to measure how the process of integration develops, peaks and declines (see Figure 1.2 in Chapter 1). The "quantification" of globalization, its extent and penetration make it possible to understand how the process itself develops.

Measurement is essential, first of all, to comprehend the effective diffusion of the integration processes in purely geographic terms. If the current globalization wave is undoubtedly made up of a number of "global planetary events" (for instance, the recent COVID-19 pandemic), the idea of a fully globalized world is nevertheless debatable, debated and widely criticized. This is evident on looking further back at the more distant past, for instance at the integration waves which have punctuated world history since the late Middle Ages.

This chapter aims to provide an overview of the way in which the processes of globalization have been measured by social scientists, from the waves of integration that developed in the past up to the most recent and sophisticated efforts to develop comprehensive globalization indices accounting for the acceleration of integration.

Globalization is an extremely complex phenomenon in which many events and dynamics occur at the same time in different spheres of human activity. As Chapter 2 showed when narrating the history of the 19th-century globalization wave, large areas of economic, political and social action are simultaneously invested by globalization or de-globalization processes; simultaneity makes a univocal measurement of these phenomena extremely difficult.

One way to proceed is, therefore, to agree on a proper definition of globalization, in order to disentangle its components which may then be

DOI: 10.4324/9780429490255-3

appropriately quantified. Two examples can be used here: the debates as to the extent of globalization and its birthdate.

3.1.1 Flat or spiky? The extent of globalization

The first debate concerns the effective "outreach" of globalization. At what was probably the peak of the second globalization wave in the early 2000s, Thomas Friedman argued in an international bestseller (*The World Is Flat: A Brief History of the Twenty-first Century*, 2005) that the world had become "flat" due to an ongoing intense revolution in information and communication technology, and to the economic policies pursued by governments, which enabled an unprecedented time-space compression of economic dynamics. One of the main implications of this assumption is that the world could be considered as a leveled field on which all players enjoy equal opportunities.

The generally positive reception of Friedman's book was swiftly accompanied by a vivid discussion and several criticisms, which provided plenty of data and examples to prove that the world was not at all "flat". Richard Florida's article "The World Is Spiky" (2005) soon offered new empirical data on variables, such as the distribution of the world's population, light emissions, patents and scientific citations. The article suggested that the international economic landscape was not at all flat by almost any measure. On the contrary, the world still looked amazingly "spiky". For instance, the distribution of the world's population was very uneven, economic activity approximated from light emission data was significantly concentrated in a few areas, the world production of innovation measured by patents issued was also concentrated in a very few places, and the world's most influential scientific researchers were mostly in the US and Europe.

Further investigations in the following years revealed a world that was only a fraction as integrated as had been thought. According to Pankaj Ghemawat (2007), the level of internationalization associated with cross-border migration, telephone calls, management research, direct investment, private charitable donations, patenting, portfolio investment and trade was much nearer to 10 percent of GDP than to 100 percent, except for international trade, which stood at around 20 percent (Table 3.1). These numbers would imply a relatively low level of global integration.

The world was thus stated to be "curvy" rather than flat, meaning that the world economy in the late 2000s showed trends toward increasing globalization and toward a persistent local orientation. For instance, while the real transport costs of shipping products or information might have dropped dramatically, this might not be true for the transaction costs involved in the exchange, which could be strongly influenced by local market specificities.

Table 3.1 Levels of internationalization across industries

Category	%
Immigration (to population)	2
Phone call revenues	4
Management research	6
Direct investment	7
Private charity	8
Management cases	10
Patents	12
Portfolio investment	13
Trade	23

Source: Authors' elaboration on Ghemawat (2007), p. 56.

3.1.2 Globalization: one or many?

A second challenging debate concerns the identification of the birthdate of globalization; or rather, its *birthdates*. Historians have identified at least three turning points in the Christian Era which can be considered opportune "watersheds", phases characterized by an acceleration of the integration process. The beginning of the second millennium (1000 CE) could definitely be considered an appropriate "starting point", since the world had by then evolved from a condition in which the most important aspects shaping human life and social institutions led to completely separate social aggregations; it was a world in which societies increasingly functioned as a result of contacts, communications, interactions and imitative practices. This view is strongly supported by data such as the numbers of wide-ranging inter-regional journeys, the availability of accurate maps, the transfer of technological know-how, and to a minor extent by consumer tastes and an increasing dependence on long-distance trade. In addition, recent discoveries of shipwrecks tell the story of intensifying interaction between very distant parts of the world even before the year 1000. There is, for instance, the case of the Arab dhow that sank around 825 near the island of Beitlung (today's Indonesia) with its multiracial and multireligious crew. The ship had discharged its merchandise from the Near East, probably spices, pearls, precious stones, metals and textiles. It had taken on another cargo in the port of Guangzhou, and then sank on its return journey to the Abbasid Empire. Archeologists investigating the shipwrecked dhow found nearly 70,000 pieces of ceramics, which had been mass-produced in China's Hunan province for export to foreign markets, in addition to gold and silver ornaments, mirrors, incense burners, bottles and two objects that may have been children's toys. The ship had almost certainly intended to pause its journey at the midway point in Southeast Asia to unload part of its cargo and pick up an additional cargo of spices, resins and aromatics.

A few centuries later, the start of the 16th century can rightly be considered another "turning point" in the process of social, commercial and cultural integration. New dynamics moved the world closer to globalization. According to some economic historians, for instance, it can be claimed that, following a path-dependent process from previous centuries, which continued during subsequent centuries, globalization began around the year 1571, when Manila was founded as a Spanish *entrepôt* and direct and permanent connections were established between Europe, the Americas and East Asia. Scholars have based their position on the analysis of different categories of aspects: biological and demographical dynamics, like the emergence of a global disease pool following the transmission of European and African diseases in the Americas; aspects of culture, like the global spread of fashion items such as Indian chintz cloth; and some economic trends, like the remarkable increase in international trade. All these facets and their possible measurements are better described in the next section.

Chapter 2 of this book describes in depth the other possible birthdate of globalization, the phase following the conclusion of the Napoleonic Wars. Restricting the definition of "globalization" to "the integration of the international commodity market", some economic historians are adamant in stating that a globalization wave began during the early decades of the 19th century, and not before then. In their opinion, the irrefutable evidence that globalization was taking place is provided by an observable decline in the international dispersion of commodity prices, or rather, by the convergence of commodity prices, something never seen in previous centuries. As far as grain market integration is concerned, for instance, Kevin O'Rourke and Jeffrey Williamson compared prices in Liverpool, Britain's most important grain trading port, and in Chicago, the city closest to America's grain producers. According to their estimates, Liverpool prices exceeded Chicago prices by 60.3 percent around 1870, falling to 25.4 percent around 1895, and 14.9 percent around 1912. A similar trend can also be seen for other commodities. For example, prices of pig iron in Philadelphia exceeded London prices by 75 percent around 1870, by 43.3 percent around 1895, and by 20.6 percent around 1913 (O'Rourke and Williamson, 1994, pp. 899 and 900).

This summary is not an appropriate place for detailed discussion of the debates surrounding the many possible birthdates of globalization. Nevertheless, the different positions that scholars have taken make it evident that the differing views on globalization, its dynamics and its impact depend on different definitions of the phenomenon, and on different measurements of globalization.

Which variables should then be considered in measuring the process of global integration? Which level or threshold should these variables reach to make it possible to claim that we are entering (or leaving) a globalization dynamic? Which data (if available) should be used to quantify these variables? Should we look at globalization "from the top" by asking how much the world as a whole is "globalized", or "from the bottom" by looking at the level of inclusion and participation of each single country or geographical area in the global economic system? Which percentage of the world would have to be involved in some form of integration, and to what extent, to make it possible to talk of a "globalized world"? Despite its complex and multifaceted nature, scholars in several fields of social sciences accepted the challenge of proposing a measure of globalization, and in some cases of its impact. The following section of this chapter will provide an overview of the sources and measurements of globalization at our disposal in the long term, while the last section will focus on the contemporary dynamics of globalization.

3.2 Globalization measured: the distant past

As might be expected, the attempt to measure globalization from a historical perspective is made even more challenging by the lack of reliable historical sources, which could be literally unavailable for several components of the process itself, for distant historical periods and for certain geographic areas. Nevertheless, historians have proposed tentative measures of globalization in the long term, using a combination of both qualitative and quantitative approaches. In some cases, scholars have also made some attempts to measure certain specific aspects of globalization, such as time-space compression, showing the multitude of ways human beings have tried to bridge distances more rapidly and to exchange goods and information more efficiently.

It is, of course, impossible to offer even an approximate account of the quantitative relevance of integration in the pre-industrial era. For the pre-industrial period, identification of the origins of globalization and analysis of "globalization waves" are usually based on the collection of empirical evidence of increasing intensity in exchanges and flows at a world level, rather than on a quantification of the "extent" of globalization in a specific time frame, given the almost complete absence of historical indexes of globalization.

3.2.1 Measurements in ancient history

Historians have sought information about exchanges among peoples of different geographic areas even before the availability of written sources. Archeologists have traced migration patterns that brought people to new areas, obtaining information on the earliest long-distance trading activities. For example, their findings demonstrate that shells from the Indian Ocean had reached Syria by approximately 5000 BCE, and there is also evidence of crop exchange between the Persian Gulf region and Africa's east coast in around 4000 BCE.

The invention of writing provides more reliable information, allowing closer observation of economic and cultural exchanges among peoples. The Babylonian epic poem *Gilgamesh* is based on the story of a king who travels to find timber for his palace, and the Hindu holy book the *Rig Veda* describes an Indian merchant ship being attacked by pirates in the Persian Gulf; both books tell of early long-distance trade and interaction. In the era of the great classical civilizations, empires began to create institutional and physical infrastructures that allowed them to have contacts with each other.

There is also plenty of anecdotal evidence of some forms of tourist activity in ancient times. The first list of the famous "Seven Wonders of the World" was drawn up by the historian Herodotus in the 5th century BCE. In the following centuries, the spread of universal religions helped to keep contacts alive in a framework in which old empires dissolved. Recent discoveries of shipwrecks like the Arab dhow prove the variety and extent of long-distance trade between the Middle East and China, while the activity of mapping the known world became increasingly detailed and sophisticated around the end of the first and the start of the second millennium. Over time, cultural and technological exchanges started to emerge more clearly. Although archeologists and written sources provide evidence of a world in which there were some contacts between geographically distant areas, most interactions took place among neighboring regions. "Regionalization of exchange flows" would be a more appropriate term to describe these "proto-globalization" dynamics.

3.2.2 From the Middle Ages to the early modern period

It would be difficult for anyone to succeed in accurately quantifying global flows and interactions before the 11th or the 16th century. However, the evidence at our disposal, which is based on essays, diaries, and manuals, allows us to "measure" some aspects that might have favored long-distance trade and flows of people from the turn of the first millennium. For instance, it is known that between 1318 and 1559, Venetian merchant galleys increased in length from 27.8 to 40.4 meters, in width from 5.3 to 8 meters, in depth from 2.4 to 3.1 meters and in cargo capacity from 110 to 280 metric tons (Maddison, 2010, p. 56). At the same time, the sources document real travels over very long distances, such as those of Ibn Battuta or Marco Polo, something for which there is no evidence during the previous centuries. Historians describe how some regions began to look at others, activating institutional, cultural and technological learning processes.

As suggested above, several scholars argue that the first global economy dates back to the 16th century. They base their theses on three broad categories of biological, cultural and economic data (more specifically trade-related). Firstly, as far as biological data are concerned, the level of globalization could be reflected in the spread of contagious diseases like the bubonic plague of the 14th century, which originated in Asia and spread throughout the Middle East, northern Africa, Italy, and the rest of Europe, or else the European and African diseases that spread in the Americas from the end of the 15th century. The disease pool became global, and by the 19th century, everyone in the world, with a few exceptions, had "absorbed" the same mix of diseases, and developed similar immunities. The existence of something close to a "global space" is also reflected in other biological indicators like the exchange of foodstuffs. Although food exchanges date back to much more ancient times, the addition of the Americas made it possible to create a new and more varied diet that became global in the space of a few centuries.

Furthermore, the extent of globalization since the 16th century can also be analyzed by looking at cultural dynamics. Books and the press spread from Europe to its colonies, bringing intellectual ideas and scientific information. This gave origin to an international intellectual community that could take advantage of the dissemination of various kinds of knowledge across borders.

Contacts and potential exchanges increased over time, driving an intensification of mutual cultural influences, but also provoking an open or implicit reaction in some areas against too much cultural connection in defense of local identity. Global contacts pushed some countries to exclude outside influences, as in the cases of China and Japan. The multiplication of contacts with Europeans and their increasing influence led to rising hostility against foreigners in the Celestial Empire during the 15th century. Chinese Emperor Xuande intended to close his country off from the rest of the world with the Edict of Haijin (1434). Trade and interaction with the outside world were forbidden, the official reason being widespread acts of piracy against Chinese merchant ships. In Japan, the arrival of the Portuguese in 1543 and the consequent establishment of Christian schools paved the way for the spread of European civilization in the country. In reaction, the shogunate adopted an isolationist foreign policy. As anticipated in Chapter 2, this was the *sakoku* (literally "locked country") period, which lasted from the early 1600s to the late 1800s; the government prohibited foreign travel, European visitors and Christian religious practices, and placed severe restrictions on international trade.

According to some historians, another important cultural trend strictly related to globalization is the diffusion of a new kind of consumerism from the early 16th century. As noted by Canadian historian Timothy Brooks, artists like Dutch master Jan Vermeer quickly incorporated into their portraits and paintings the ongoing process of integration via an intense exchange of consumer goods between the increasingly affluent Western European bourgeoisie and nobility and the opulent and fascinating territories of the East Indies.

Data on international trade are frequently cited by historians of the modern age to argue that globalization started in the 16th century. This could be acceptable if adhering to a sharply focused definition of globalization, namely the presence and increasing denseness of permanent trade flows between distant regions of the globe, with all the main areas of the world exchanging products continuously on a scale generating deep and lasting impacts on all trading partners (Flynn and Giráldez, 2004). It is now widely recognized by historians that by the mid-17th century, three intercontinental, long-distance trade systems had become consolidated: a Eurasian, an Atlantic and a Pacific system.

The main protagonists of this long-distance trade were the "chartered companies", state-sponsored trading firms, whose reports are a valuable source of precious information, mainly from the letters and other written documents exchanged between the foreign branches abroad and their offices in the countries of origin. One of the largest chartered companies, the British East India Company, was constantly updated about its trading activities via regional reports. Its accounting records provide detailed data regarding sales and inventories. Starting from this period of history, these sources and the other information available make it relatively easy to obtain more quantitative evidence on trade and trade-related activities and indirectly provide some hints that help us understand the extent and direction of supranational trade flows. There is a wealth of data, particularly on the numbers and the destination of fleets, the size and capacity of ships, and the number of products that were traded, especially gold and silver. These data tell us, for instance, that the number of ships sailing to Asia from European countries like Portugal, the Netherlands, England, France, Sweden and Denmark rose from 770 in the 16th century to 6,661 in the 18th century, and that in the same period the average capacity of ships increased from 300 to 1,000 metric tons. The cargo capacity of the Dutch fleet rose from 60,000 metric tons in 1470 to 140,000 metric tons in 1824, while the capacity of the British fleet grew sharply from 51,000 metric tons in 1570 to 1 million metric tons in 1780 (Maddison, 2010, pp. 65–66).

Information is available about some specific trade dynamics like the boom in European intercontinental exchanges between 1500 and 1800. According to O'Rourke and Williamson, whatever unit of measurement is considered (tonnage, number or value), European intercontinental and world trade began to grow from the 16th century. Their work makes it possible to estimate this growth and assess the heterogeneous paths followed by different routes, products and countries (O'Rourke and Williamson, 2002). Table 3.2 is based on a selection of some of their estimates, and this allows us, for instance, to evaluate the average trend in European intercontinental trade, to assess the trade balance and intensity of growth in different routes, and also to observe the ascent and decline of some of the main protagonists, such as the Portuguese who traded with Asia.

Table 3.2 European intercontinental and world trade growth (growth per annum – percentages)

	1500–1549	1550–1599	1600–1649	1650–1699	1700–1749	1750–1799
Average	2.42	0.12	0.75	0.55	1.33	1.17
Portugal to/ from Asia (tonnage)	1.37	0.94	−3.36	0.25	n.a.	n.a.
Dutch East India to Asia (tonnage)	n.a.	n.a.	1.62	0.48	1.07	−1.10
Dutch East India from Asia (tonnage)	n.a.	n.a.	2.17	0.63	1.20	−1.43
English tobacco imports from America (kilos)	n.a.	n.a.	0.12	2.83	1.80	n.a.
Sugar exports from Spanish colonies (pounds)	n.a.	−6.11	0.15	−3.83	4.63	−0.46
Irish exports to American colonies (£)	n.a.	n.a.	n.a.	n.a.	2.15	2.69

Source: Adapted from O'Rourke and Williamson (2002), pp. 419–420.

3.3 The late modern and contemporary eras

3.3.1 *Measuring the economic aspects of globalization*

There is plenty of evidence that trade links have drawn closer during the modern period as civilizations continued their pattern of integration. As mentioned above, it is almost impossible to provide an accurate measurement of what we call "globalization" in the centuries before the First Industrial Revolution due to the persistent and structural discontinuities in data series, which enable only discontinuous analysis and observation of very general trends. The century that for the first time, according to several scholars, welcomed a truly globalized world was also the one in which more information and more reliable data started to become available. Therefore, attempts to measure global dynamics are more frequent and more accurate when scholars analyze the 19th and 20th centuries. Economic historians have been able to successfully measure the extent of globalization and achieve a better understanding of its dynamics through proxies like data on international trade, international flows of capital and cross-border migrations. Other attempts have been made to measure the integration of markets across space in the long term, and to provide empirical evidence about other non-economic features of globalization, such as its cultural and institutional impacts and, in a few cases, also suggest some quantitative measures.

Quantitative indicators of globalization measure the size of international flows of commodities and factors in either absolute or relative terms. Access to reliable information greatly depends on the historical period and the availability of appropriate sources in different geographic locations. Investigations of the 19th and 20th centuries have focused particularly on measuring the flows of goods (international trade), capital (international investment) and people (international migration).

The first of these, international trade, has been analyzed in considerable depth during recent decades. Statistical accounts became increasingly accurate after the Second World War, and data published by the World Trade Organization nowadays make it possible to reconstruct trade flows and their composition with a great degree of precision. Based on sources at a country level (normally, national historical accounts), historians have obtained information on the trading activities of single nations and, in some cases, have built up long-term series in order to measure international trade flows in the last few centuries. Inspiring studies in this field allow us not only to appreciate the main trends in international trade, especially the quantity and variety of imports and exports of each country and their transformation over time, but also to understand the main dynamics behind these trends, to reconstruct patterns in commercial openness, and to analyze the impact that international trade could have had on other variables of economic development.

Ronald Findlay and Kevin O'Rourke provide an account of world trade and development over the entire course of the last millennium (Findlay and O'Rourke, 2007). Drawing on their own original empirical research and extensive analysis of secondary sources, they reconstruct the main trends in international trade, examining their origins, dynamics and consequences for world economic development. The level of accuracy of their work can, of course, increase when dealing with recent centuries. As far as the first half of the millennium is concerned, for instance, they focus on how the *Pax Mongolica*, which bound together most of the Eurasian landmass under the Mongol Empire in the 14th century, favored both long-distance trade and the diffusion of a "microbial common market". According to Findlay and O'Rourke, these dynamics set the stage for a subsequent expansion of population, output and prices in some regions, and also for the launch of Iberian exploration in search of new trade routes when the *Pax Mongolica* disintegrated. In their opinion, the growth of international trade in the following centuries was one of the main trends that preceded and favored the industrialization process, before the actual Industrial Revolution occurred and set in motion economic forces that shaped the extent and dynamics of international trade during the 19th and 20th centuries. This then caused an international specialization of countries, which counterposed a core of industrial nations and a peripheral set of primary producing nations. Findlay and O'Rourke's account of world trade dynamics and the way they are intertwined with global economic and political development continues in the same vein with their analysis of the establishment and disintegration of the *Pax Britannica* of the 19th century and of the *Pax Americana* of the second half of the 20th century.

The second aspect of globalization that is increasingly quantifiable with data covering the last century and a half is foreign direct investment in the form of the capital invested abroad in income-generating assets. There was a significant improvement in the possibility of quantifying international flows of capital after the Second World War, when supranational institutions began the systematical collection of data. In this sense, the reports of the United Nations Conference on Trade and Development (UNCTAD) are particularly important. In some cases, national sources allow researchers to quantify flows of capital to and from specific locations in the last two or three decades of the 19th century. Of course, there is an intense debate as to the reliability of these data. In several cases it is quite difficult to distinguish between portfolio and direct investments. Also, estimates are hampered by the large percentage of investments located abroad but in the colonies of an empire, which gives them a rather uncertain status.

The third component of globalization that scholars have attempted to systematically quantify since the 19th century is migration flows. Also in this case, when national statistics, censuses and secondary sources are available, these are the main sources for historians until supranational institutions established after the Second World War began collecting international statistics and censuses. From the mid-19th century onward, reliable estimates are now available on the origin, destination (at a macro-region level) and overall number of migrants of the major long-distance migration flows.

Antunes and Fatah-Black (2016) provide a good synthesis of measurements of these three elements in the long term, almost up to the peak of the Second Globalization at the start of the 21st century, with an overview of these metrics and their transformation over time (Table 3.3).

According to these data, and coherently with what has been described in Chapter 2, there is a clear trend in global integration of both commodities and capital markets that becomes quite evident from the last few decades of the 19th century and from those of the early 20th century. On the contrary, a very clear de-globalization process is evident in the phase lasting from the First World War until the 1950s. A similar trend can also be detected for international migrations.

During recent decades, as previously mentioned, scholars have worked hard not only to quantify flows and stocks of goods, capital and people, but also to investigate whether there was a convergence in prices of goods and costs of factors, meaning the integration of commodity markets, labor and capital markets. In fact, although rough data on the volume of trade, flows of capital and international migrations are informative, they do not actually prove that the markets were effectively integrated with each other. For instance, the volume of trade could increase or decrease for reasons unrelated to market integration or disintegration, such as shifts in supply and demand that are not necessarily connected to globalization. On the other hand, gaps in commodity prices and factors of production reflect all relevant elements of the costs of trading and transferring capital and labor, such as transportation costs, political barriers (such as tariffs and non-tariff trade barriers) and wars. At the same time, the convergence of prices among different areas of the world in different historical periods would effectively prove their ongoing integration.

Data showing market integration are still limited, but their quality is improving with time, and several studies on this topic have been published in the last two decades. According to these, an accelerating trend toward global integration of markets of capitals, labor and technology can be detected from

Table 3.3 Quantity-based indicators of economic globalization

	1870	1913	1929	1950	1973	1998
Merchandise exports (% of world GDP)	4.6	7.9	9.0	5.5	10.5	17.2

	1870	1914	1930	1945	1960	1980	1990	1995	2001
Foreign assets/world GDP	0.07	0.18 (0.22)	0.08	0.05	0.06	0.25	0.49	0.62	(0.75)

Net migration (1,000s)	1870–1913	1914–1949	1950–1973	1974–1998
Old World (includes France, Germany, Italy, Japan, the UK, Belgium, the Netherlands, Sweden and Switzerland)	−13,996	−3,662	9,381	10,898
New World (includes Australia, New Zealand, Canada and the US)	17,856	7,239	12,663	21,639

Sources: Cátia Antunes and Karwan Fatah-Black, in turn based on: A. Maddison, *The World Economy: Historical Statistics*. Paris: OECD, 2010; Maurice Obstfeld and Alan M. Taylor, "Globalization and Capital Markets", in Michael D. Bordo, Alan M. Taylor and Jeffrey G. Williamson (eds.), *Globalization in Historical Perspective*. Chicago, IL: University of Chicago Press, 2003: 121–188; Moritz Schularick, "A Tale of Two 'Globalizations': Capital Flows from Rich to Poor in Two Eras of Global Finance", *International Journal of Finance & Economics*, Volume 11, Issue 4, 2006: 339–354; Hania Zlotnik "International Migration 1965–1996: An Overview", *Population and Development Review*, Volume 24, Issue 3, 1998: 429–468; Richard B. Freeman, "People Flows in Globalization", *Journal of Economic Perspectives*, Volume 20, Issue 2, 2006: 145–170.

the start of the 19th century. Although this approach has been criticized as being insufficient to account for global transformation, these analyses still make a remarkable effort in attempting to measure at least some of the relevant dynamics of economic globalization, if not the phenomenon as a whole.

As far as commodity market integration is concerned, scholars have shown that there is abundant evidence of a very intense globalization process that had begun to unfold by the 1820s, after the Napoleonic Wars. Findlay and O'Rourke showed that the variety of goods traded between continents had steadily increased over time since the end of the 15th century, resulting in clear integration of the commodity market. For instance, Federico et al. (2021) show that convergence of prices in the wheat market was a predominantly pre-modern phenomenon. However, this became especially apparent when driven by politics and technology during the 19th and 20th centuries. It has been shown that commodity price gaps between continents fell by four-fifths overall between 1820 and 1914, primarily due to lower transport costs. Here, it should also be stressed that the trend in price convergence of commodities was not monotonic, but was periodically interrupted by shocks like world depressions and wars, or by domestic national political responses to the impact of globalization on income distribution.

As far as the integration of capital markets is concerned, while the major financial centers in the 17th and 18th centuries, London and Amsterdam, were well integrated with each other, the situation of the smaller centers was different. The extent of integration of capital markets increased in the era of the International Gold Standard, approximately five decades before the First World War. This trend was abruptly halted by the First World War and by the barriers that constrained international flows of capital in the following decades. It would only start up again with the collapse of the Bretton Woods system in the early 1970s, resulting in the free transfer of capital among countries. The efficiency of capital markets, usually based on arbitrage that reduces price differences between similar assets, in this case interest rates, also depended on the fact that there were no restrictions on capital mobility. Estimates for the US and Europe show that interest rates were converging on zero before the First World War and again after the 1980s, indicating that the capital market was efficient; since investors were free to borrow in the cheapest places, this made interest rates increase and caused the reduction or end of the interest rate gap. On the other hand, from the interwar years to the 1970s, large interest rate differentials were the norm, showing that the financial markets had low levels of integration and efficiency (Obstfeld and Taylor, 2003).

Last but not least, labor market integration has been measured by looking at the convergence of real wages, the variable with the lowest degree of convergence, even in phases of global economic integration. Real wages should – in theory – converge among different geographic locations, since labor should move freely from countries with an excess of labor and low wages to nations with a higher demand for labor and higher wages. Nevertheless, empirical evidence proves that although wage differentials between countries have been powerful drivers of migration flows, migration barriers and the differences in labor productivity between different areas actually reduced the impact of these dynamics during the 19th and 20th centuries, so that differences in wage levels between different countries persisted. A reduction in the real wage gap is, for instance, seen within Europe and between Europe and the US during the First Global Economy, when income gaps between rich and poor countries converged and real wage dispersion declined by over a quarter between 1870 and 1910, and again after 1950. However, a similar trend cannot be detected between developed and developing countries in the same period.

3.3.2 Globalization and culture

Besides its impacts on the economic sphere, globalization has been analyzed from the perspective of an ongoing convergence in non-economic variables, which are not always easy to quantify and measure. More frequently, empirical evidence of an anecdotal kind has been used. However, in some cases, scholars have tried to quantify some cultural elements that are useful for understanding the impact of globalization on cultural attitudes.

Cultural globalization is a very broad concept, which refers to the transmission of ideas, meanings and values around the world in such a way as to expand and strengthen social relations. Therefore, it is a field of research for several disciplines, including anthropology, sociology, cultural studies, geography and political science, all with their different approaches and methods.

Measurements of cultural globalization usually relate to what are considered its main drivers, such as communications or media, or relate to the transformation of cultural dynamics themselves, which can be reflected in languages, religions, and the consumption of material and immaterial goods like food, fashion, sport or movies. The establishment of both national and supranational institutions might also be related, at least partly, to dynamics of cultural globalization and imitation. Although the size of the topic makes it impossible to deal exhaustively with every aspect, we can provide examples of how scholars have dealt with some of these.

For example, in order to measure the drivers of cultural globalization, scholars have tried to estimate the extent of communication networks and the spread of communication devices. In order to assess the range of the global communication system in the 19th century, historians have calculated how many kilometers of undersea telegraph cables were laid. The same method has been used to measure the extent of other communication networks and the spread of communication devices in other historical periods up to the present day. For instance, television and internet access and the spread of smartphones are today considered to be significant parameters for evaluation of the potential extent of cultural globalization.

One way that the role of the media in the process of cultural globalization has been approached in a historical perspective has been to observe and quantify the number, size and range of the first communications corporations, including international news agencies. Some examples of the earliest agencies include Agence Havas (Paris, 1835), Reuters (London, 1851) and Associated Press (New York, 1840s). Scholars have also tried to measure other aspects that are possibly important in fostering the establishment of a global culture, like the concentration rate of the global telecommunications industry. For example, it is important to know that in 2019 the world's eight largest media companies (Comcast, Disney, Alphabet, Charter Communications, AT&T, Twenty-First Century Fox, Thomson Reuters and CBS News Corporation) accounted for more than two-thirds of the revenues in the world telecommunications industry (Steger, 2020: 91).

In addition, the spread of a global culture is often measured by observing the transformation of cultural dynamics themselves. The global spread of languages and religions and trends in the consumption of goods such as food, fashion, sport or movies, are also good examples in this sense.

As far as language is concerned, the variety of languages and dialects spoken around the world has shrunk considerably in recent centuries. Approximately 14,500 languages were spoken in the world in the early 16th century; the number had fallen to 12,000 by the early 18th century, to 10,000 by the early 19th, to 7,500 by the early 20th, and to just 2,997 by the early 21st (Steger, 2020, p. 92). This could be due to many factors, such as the progressive expansion of national education systems. Some scholars, however, suggest a correlation between the growing global importance of a few languages, especially English, Spanish and Chinese, and the falling number of other languages around the world. What is certain is the remarkable global spread of these few languages. In the late 16th century, for instance, in the early stages of British colonialism, only approximately 1 percent of the world population used English as their mother tongue. At the end of the 20th century, this percentage had increased to 6 percent, and an additional 7 percent of the world population used English as a second language.

A second aspect of cultural globalization is related to religious dynamics. Going back to the Crusades and earlier, religion and globalization proved to be closely connected. Samuel Huntington claimed that at the end of the 20th century, the major religions had spread around the world: Christianity turning "southern" and "black", Islam turning "Asian", and Buddhism turning "white" and "Western" (Huntington, 1993). Measuring the spread of a religion is a very difficult task. For example, counting the members of a religious group involves difficult issues, the first of which is how to define which features and behaviors make an individual a "member" of that group. Nevertheless, significant efforts have been made to estimate how widespread each religion in the world is in the long term. The World Religion Database, edited by Todd Johnson and Brian Grim, contains detailed statistics on religious affiliations for every country of the world from the beginning of the 20th century.[1] Another example is provided by the Database of Religious History,[2] a Harvard University project that aims to be a comprehensive quantitative and qualitative encyclopedia of world religious history.

When looking at global trends in the consumption of material and immaterial goods, several examples could be cited regarding the spread of global standards in consumption habits, especially since the 19th century.

As far as food is concerned, empirical evidence shows how certain cuisines began to globalize following migration waves from certain areas, as with French, Italian and Chinese cuisines in the second half of the 19th century. Many histories could be written about these cases, and some attempts have been made to map the spread of restaurants of a specific cuisine in a specific city or geographical area since the 19th century. One interesting example is provided by Chinese restaurants in San Francisco, where almost all the restaurants at the beginning of the Gold Rush were run by Chinese immigrants. Most were Cantonese, and they served Western-style chops and steaks alongside fricassees and various hashes. Chinese immigrants managed a wide range of restaurants, from low-level eateries serving day workers with cheap food for a few cents to middle- and high-class places offering more variety for salaried workers, and even very expensive banquet halls. A good example of global food culture from the most recent globalization wave is the worldwide success of American fast-food chains like McDonald's. This chain is so widespread in the world that the price of one of its most iconic hamburgers, the Big Mac, has been used as an informal tool to compare purchasing power parity among world currencies (the "Big Mac Index").

Fashion and luxury consumption is another field of global cultural fusion that has attracted scholars' interest. For centuries, the long-distance trade in Eastern textiles was driven by the appeal of luxury fabrics and the Western attraction to the idea of exoticism. Looking at Europe as a trend-setter, historians have written extensively about the influence exerted by Spanish art, culture and costume on European culture in the 16th and 17th centuries. From the powerful court of the Habsburgs, the *moda a la española* spread to other European courts. Fashion historians consider Spain responsible for the spread of "solemn black" clothing throughout Europe and the New World. The Spanish monarchs who dressed with "citizen-like modesty" are deemed the precursors of the 19th century's severe bourgeois fashion in Europe and the New World. Measuring these dynamics is a very challenging task. Scholars exploring the present day concentrate on the global spread of the major players in clothing, fashion and luxury products, such as Nike, Louis Vuitton, Gucci, Chanel, Adidas, Hermès, Zara, H&M, Cartier and UNIQLO, and on their impact on global sales. Luxury is one of the most globalized businesses, with just a few multinational companies controlling global sales networks. The ten largest luxury goods firms in the late 2010s controlled almost 50 percent of the industry's global sales (Donzé and Pouillard, 2019, p. 424).

In the case of immaterial "products", the emergence of international sports organizations has been used as a unit of measurement to assess the increasing process of globalization in this field from the last decades of the 19th century. In this context, it is worth mentioning the modern Olympic Games, overseen by the International Olympic Committee that was established in 1896. This was followed a few years later, in 1902, by the International Cycling Union, and in 1904 by FIFA (Fédération Internationale de Football Association), an international organization set up to oversee and coordinate soccer games at a global level.

One example of a creative sector in the cultural goods field is the movie industry, which also reflects the dynamics of cultural globalization, both in itself and in spreading models and ways of life that may be imitated worldwide. In this case, the reference is undoubtedly "Hollywood". Business historians of the movie industry, like Peter Miskell, have reconstructed the dynamics of this sector and also provided extensive quantitative information on the international range of the large American companies in the 20th century. For example, in the mid-1920s, approximately 75 percent of the movies screened around the world were from the US. By the 1930s, eight major companies had emerged to dominate the industry (Fox, Loew's-MGM, Paramount, Warner Bros., RKO, Universal, Columbia and United Artists), and all had already invested in extensive global distribution networks. The industry further expanded abroad in the following decades and progressively increased its process of adapting contents to a foreign audience with an international production process that business historians can map and measure. In Italy, for instance, producer Dino de Laurentiis made epics like *The Bible* for Twentieth Century Fox in the 1960s. At the end of the century, the international attention of US filmmakers shifted to Asia in an attempt to develop content that appealed to both Asian and Western audiences; Ang Lee's *Crouching Tiger, Hidden Dragon* (2000) is a good example of this (Miskell, 2019).

Lastly, cultural globalization in a wide sense has also had an indirect impact on the process of imitation and contamination of institutions worldwide. According to US scholar Eleanor Westney, for instance, the import and imitation of Western institutions formed the basis of Japan's modernization process that began in the last quarter of the 19th century. This process was further accelerated by the world tour of the Iwakura Mission, the "fact-finding" initiative launched by the new Meiji government in 1877, which sent a group of diplomats and young scholars abroad to study, understand and copy Western institutional practices.

The spread of ideas at a global level can be measured indirectly by looking at the emergence and diffusion of international non-governmental organizations and global institutions during the last couple of centuries. For example, with regard to non-governmental organizations, the establishment of international non-governmental organizations increased from the 1860s, including the Workingmen's International founded by Karl Marx in 1864, while feminism began to go global in the 1880s. The idea that there were some globally applicable humanitarian standards began to transcend borders.

The origins of international institutions can be traced back to an International Postal Congress of 1863, called by the US and held in Paris, to tackle the issue of mailing letters and packages between different countries. The General Postal Union was established in 1874 and was the first of many international agreements based on the principle of coordination, including patents and intellectual property, maritime law and wartime behavior. During the interwar years, several international agencies began operating, such as the International Labor Organization and the International Chamber of Commerce. Finally, after the Second World War, two kinds of international institution transformed the framework for globalization, one in the sphere of world politics, and the other related to the world economy. One notable example is the United Nations Organization, established by 41 member states in 1945 with the aim of ensuring international peace and security, which by 2023 included 193 member states. Another notable example is the World Trade Organization, which was established in 1995 (replacing the General Agreement on Tariffs and Trade) to facilitate trade in goods, services and intellectual property among participating countries, and by 2023 had 164 members.

3.4 Quantifying the present globalization: indices and data

With regard to measurement of global integration, it is evident how much more information is available today than in the past. Still, relatively little agreement exists about how to measure this integration. As said above, since globalization is multifaceted, there is still no agreement on a single definition, so that the different indicators considered and developed in recent research reflect the many definitions of globalization that have been developed over time. Arguably, measurement of globalization's economic impact has predominated, while its political and cultural aspects have often been relatively neglected. After describing the involvement of international organizations in providing data to measure the economic aspects of globalization, the rest of this section will present the main tools used to measure globalization, stressing their strengths and weaknesses while offering some alternatives.

There have been numerous important attempts to quantify the current globalization, or at least its economic determinants, during the last few decades. In particular, some international organizations have conducted specific research and published relevant statistics and reports. Some of these aim to provide relevant information on economic measurements of globalization in the present day. These data sources contain information on international trade, flows of capital, people and technology, and also in relation to other relevant macroeconomic variables (e.g., GDP), and here it is worth mentioning the remarkable contribution of the Organization for Economic Cooperation and Development (OECD) (see various editions of the *OECD Handbook on Economic Globalization Indicators*,[3] the *OECD Benchmark Definition of Foreign Direct Investment*,[4] the *Manual on Statistics of International Trade in Services*,[5] and the *Technological Balance of Payments Manual*[6]), the World Bank (World Development Indicators[7]), UNCTAD (Trade and Development Report[8]) and the International Monetary Fund (Principal Global Indicators[9]).

Measurement of globalization via "indices" is a relatively recent practice. The indexes created by the World Markets Research Centre and the A.T. Kearney/Foreign Policy Globalization Index in the early 2000s gave rise to a new current of investigation. In this field, globalization is basically "reverse-engineered" by breaking it down into its fundamental dimensions in order to simplify the task of finding globalization's quantifiable features. On a country basis, data on the different aspects of globalization have been combined into indexes, which have become increasingly sophisticated over time. Their premise is that, given the degree of its complexity, it is not possible to obtain a comprehensive measurement of globalization directly. This can only be measured indirectly by using a large number of indicators with direct links to aspects of globalization.

The construction of an index certainly entails a series of possible problems, such as the lack of correspondence between the indicator selected and the concept to be measured, not to mention problems of inaccuracy, incongruency of information from different indicators about the same concept, lack of data, and the difficulties of deciding how many indicators to select and how much weight should be assigned to each one. Another issue is related to the unit of analysis usually considered by these indexes of globalization, namely the nation-state. Adopting a country-based perspective is quite an obvious choice, given that most statistical data are available at the national level. At the same time, however, this creates a distortive effect because it indicates *how far* single countries are integrated into a global economic space, rather than assessing the overall extent of globalization.

Of the many indexes developed at a national level in the last couple of decades, at least five should be mentioned here: the World Market Research Centre G-Index, the A.T. Kearney/Foreign Policy Magazine Globalization Index,[10] the CSGR Globalisation Index,[11] the Maastricht Globalisation Index (MGI)[12] and the KOF Globalisation Index (KOF Index).[13]

The World Market Research Centre G-Index can be considered one of the first big attempts at quantification. First calculated in 2001, it was primarily based on economic variables; these accounted for 90 percent of the index itself, with "international trade" and "services to exports" making up 70 percent of the overall index weight. The remaining 10 percent was devoted to technology (5 percent was telephone traffic and 5 percent the number of internet hosts). Limiting the index to economic data meant that a large number of countries could be included (about 185). For some of these, the index covered a period of over 30 years. While its geographic range was remarkable, some weaknesses of this index are its poor analysis of non-economic aspects and the *a priori* weights assigned to its variables, which lean strongly toward trade and exports. This choice significantly raised the scores of small trading nations with large transit volumes compared to their domestic economies, like Singapore.

The A.T. Kearney Index is one of the best-known globalization indexes. Published annually by *Foreign Policy* magazine from 2001 to 2006, this included four fundamental dimensions of globalization (economic integration, technological connectivity, personal contacts and political engagement) as measured for 62 countries. Two or more indicators were assigned to each dimension, for a total of 12 indicators (even if their number differed in different years), which in turn include one or more variables. For example, internet hosts and secure servers are included in the technological indicators;

membership in international organizations, participation in the United Nations Security Council peace-keeping missions, and in-country embassies are included in the category of political engagement; travel and tourism, international telephone traffic and cross-border transfers are included in the personal contact category, while international trade, foreign direct investment, portfolio investment, and income payments and receipts are considered in the economic category. Weights are assigned to different indicators according to theoretical considerations of the importance of each category, and economic indicators play a predominant role in determining 50 percent of the value of the overall index. The A.T. Kearney Index was the first composite indicator measuring globalization, and served as a benchmark for alternative indices. On the other hand, it was weaker than other indices in its geographic range.

The CSGR Globalisation Index was developed by Ben Lockwood and Michela Reodano at the Centre for the Study of Globalisation and Regionalisation of the University of Warwick in the UK, taking the A.T. Kearney/Foreign Policy Magazine Index as its template. It included three categories of globalization – economic, social and political globalization – measured for 119 nations. Between 1982 and 2004, each category was measured annually using a minimum of three indicators and a maximum of nine. Economic indicators included trade, foreign direct investments, portfolio investments and income, while the other variables also considered the number of books, films and newspapers. The weights of each indicator were assigned according to the statistical technique of the "principal component weighting method". In the CSGR Globalisation Index, variables measuring openness are corrected according to fixed country characteristics, such as the initial population size, the land area and whether a country is landlocked. The variables are normalized, with the advantage of enabling comparisons over time for a given country or between countries. However, the main disadvantage of normalization is that when additional years of data are added to the database, the maximum or minimum value of a variable may change, thus changing a country's scores (and possibly position in the ranking) for previous years.

The Maastricht Globalisation Index was calculated for 2000, 2008 and 2012. It included the political, economic, sociocultural, technological and ecological dimensions of globalization, measured via the following indicators: embassies, organizations and military for the political domain; trade, foreign direct investment and capital for the economic domain; migrants and tourism for the social and cultural domain; telephones and internet for the technological domain; and eco-footprint for the ecological domain. The inclusion of an environmental dimension is certainly a strength of this index. On the other hand, it covers only three years. The index also suggests that the world's top ten most globalized countries are in Europe, raising some doubts that the results may be due to the process of regionalization rather than to globalization.

Lastly, the KOF Globalisation Index, first created by Axel Dreher in 2002 and revised in the following years, is considered to provide one of the most significant measurements of globalization, offering information from 1970 to the present (Dreher et al., 2008). This is a composite index that measures globalization for 195 countries in the world on a scale of 1 (least globalized) to 100 (most globalized). It includes the economic dimension, which considers economic flows of trade and capital and state-imposed restrictions on these flows; the social dimension, which includes interpersonal contact, information flows and cultural aspects of globalization; and the political dimension, which includes information like the number of embassies, together with international non-governmental organizations (NGOs) and participation in United Nations peace-keeping missions. A revised version of the index also distinguishes between *de facto* and *de jure* measures for each of the different measures of globalization. While *de facto* globalization measures actual international flows and activities, *de jure* globalization measures policies and conditions, such as tariffs, which – in principle – have an impact on flows and activities. Overall, the index is based on 43 different variables, and is thus an extremely comprehensive indicator, allowing for very large-scale comparisons and analysis of a great number of countries, and over several decades. The disadvantages of using the KOF Index are common among other globalization indexes, like the possible presence of bias (for example, the over-representation of smaller countries at the top of scale), or the underestimation of informal or illegal dynamics (from shared internet connection to large sectors of the informal economy, illegal migration and so on).

Figure 3.1 shows the KOF Index trends from 1970 to 2020 considering overall world dynamics. Figure 3.1a compares *de jure* and *de facto* globalization. Figures 3.1b, 3.1c and 3.1d, on the other hand, enable assessment of the importance of economic, social and political globalization in the entire trend. The same operation can be repeated for the individual countries, and it is also possible to compare countries or to further analyze in greater detail the dynamics of specific categories of sub-periods and sub-variables.

More recently, alternative globalization indexes have been developed by non-Western institutions. It is worth mentioning here, for instance, the New Index of Globalization calculated in 2019 by Hyeon-Seung Huh and Cyn-Young Park (Asian Development Bank).[14] The index used data for 158 economies over the period 2006–2014 and included different categories (trade and investment integration, money and financial integration, value chain, infrastructure and connectivity, movement of people, and institutional and social integration)

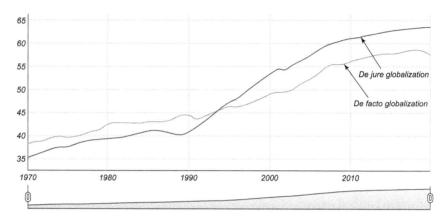

Figure 3.1a KOF Index: *de facto* and *de jure* globalization, world, 1970–2020.

measured via 25 indicators. Unlike the other indexes elaborated previously, this index makes it possible to separate the contributions of intraregional and extraregional integration.

Finally, several other indicators have been developed with the aim of giving greater weight to sociological and cultural aspects of globalization. One famous example in this sense is the GlobalIndex elaborated by Marcel Raab et al.[15] Drawing inspiration from the indexes described above, this basically aimed at replicating the KOF Globalisation Index and supplementing it with additional indicators related to socio-technical interconnectedness and to cultural globalization. GlobalIndex covered the development of globalization in 97 different countries from 1970 to 2002. Another example is the Cultural

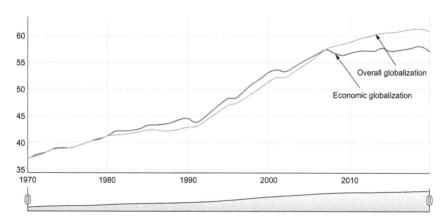

Figure 3.1b KOF Index: economic and overall globalization, world, 1970–2020.

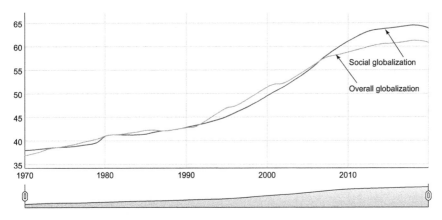

Figure 3.1c KOF Index: social and overall globalization, world, 1970–2020.

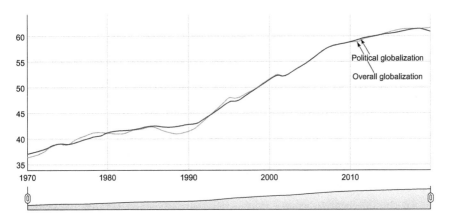

Figure 3.1d KOF Index: political and overall globalization, world, 1970–2020.

Source: KOF Globalisation Index webpage, consulted on March 25, 2023 (https://kof.ethz.ch/en/forecasts-and-indicators/indicators/kof-globalisation-index.html).

Globalization Index[16] of Kluver and Fu, which in 2004 measured the global spread of ideas by trade in media-related goods between countries. They created a ranking of the 20 most culturally globalized countries by measuring each nation's imports of books, periodicals and newspapers.

Altogether, these tools provide significant insights into quantitative measures of globalization in some of its more quantifiable variables, making it possible to compare different countries to a certain extent, and in some cases also over years or decades. However, they have also been criticized. Among their main weaknesses, it has been pointed out that the classification of countries according to the level of globalization achieved is not always congruent among different indexes. There is an issue regarding data availability and quality; so much time is needed to gather information on so many indicators that this translates into a delay in the publication of results, which are not systematically updated on the current level of globalization. Lastly, the same fact of using nation-states as a unit of analysis for a phenomenon like globalization, which basically dissolves states and their boundaries, has been heavily criticized, so alternative measurement methods have been proposed. One example in this respect is provided by Peter J. Taylor, who developed a "city-based approach" with various instruments to measure globalization from this starting point, such as "Global Network Connectivity", "Bank Network Connectivity", the "Index of NGO Network Connectivity" and "Media Network Connectivity". A.T. Kearney and *Foreign Policy* also developed a Global City Index, which includes the five dimensions of business activity (30 percent of the value of the index), human capital (30 percent), information exchange (15 percent), cultural experience (15 percent) and political engagement (10 percent), in order to measure the globalization levels of the world's major cities.

Moreover, "individual-based approaches" have also been developed recently. Caselli suggested that a person-based Globalization Index should be developed that takes into account six main dimensions: possession of the resources and the abilities necessary to move and act in the global scenario; effective mobility and activity in supranational and tendentially global domains; belonging and a sense of belonging to global, or non-territorial entities; exposure to global flows of mass communication; participation in global or supranational communication flows; and degree of global consciousness (Caselli, 2013).

All the different tools and approaches that have been created to measure globalization in the long term up to the present day have been based on different ideas of what globalization actually means, and obviously also on the availability of data. The heterogeneity of measurement systems and tools, and the different outcomes of different indicators, prove that there is not as yet one single indicator capable of measuring the complex and multidimensional process of globalization. The tools thus far elaborated can allow us to comprehend some dynamics of globalization and the intensity of some of its dimensions (especially where flows are concerned), but they cannot measure the entire phenomenon in a comprehensive and satisfactory way.

Notes

1 https://www.worldreligiondatabase.org/.
2 https://religiondatabase.org/.
3 https://www.oecd-ilibrary.org/economics/measuring-globalisation-oecd-hand-book-on-economic-globalisation-indicators-2005_9789264108103-en.

4 https://www.oecd.org/investment/fdibenchmarkdefinition.htm.
5 https://www.oecd.org/sdd/its/manualonstatisticsofinternationaltradeinservices
   .htm.
6 https://www.oecd-ilibrary.org/science-and-technology/proposed-standard
   -method-of-compiling-and-interpreting-technology-balance-of-payments-data
   _9789264065567-en.
7 https://databank.worldbank.org/source/world-development-indicators
8 https://unctad.org/tdr2022.
9 https://www.econdb.com/dataset/IMF_PGI/?FREQ=[Q]&INDICATOR=
   [FSANL_PT]&REF_AREA=[ID]&UNIT_MULT=[0]&from=2017-01-01&h=
   TIME&mode=Table&to=2020-05-01&v=Reference+Area.
10 https://foreignpolicy.com/2009/10/29/measuring-globalization-rankings/.
11 https://warwick.ac.uk/fac/soc/pais/research/csgr/index/.
12 https://cris.maastrichtuniversity.nl/en/publications/the-maastricht-globalisa-
   tion-index-an-update.
13 https://kof.ethz.ch/en/forecasts-and-indicators/indicators/kof-globalisation
   -index.html.
14 https://www.adb.org/sites/default/files/publication/513856/ewp-587-new
   -index-globalization.pdf.
15 https://journals.sagepub.com/doi/10.1177/0268580908090729.
16 https://foreignpolicy.com/2004/02/10/the-cultural-globalization-index/?gclid
   =Cj0KCQjwt_qgBhDFARIsABcDjOcoZ4t-Jmd2m9aWc0z2u4IJDLlxv4_v74
   Ytx2AGOWhDsSnaH824yD8aAvPdEALw_wcB.

References

Cátia Antunes and Karwan Fatah-Black (eds.), *Explorations in History and Globalization*. London: Routledge, 2016.

Michael D. Bordo, Alan M. Taylor, and Jeffrey G. Williamson (eds.), *Globalization in Historical Perspective*. Chicago: The University of Chicago Press, 2003.

Marco Caselli, "Nation states, cities, and people: Alternative ways to measure globalization", *SAGE Open*, 3(4), 2013. https://journals.sagepub.com/doi/full/10.1177/2158244013508417

Pierre-Yves Donzé and Véronique Pouillard, "Luxury", in Teresa da Silva Lopes, Christina Lubinski, and Heidi J.S. Tworek (eds.), *The Routledge Companion to the Makers of Global Business*. London: Routledge, 2019: 424–237.

Axel Dreher, Noel Gaston, and Pim Martens, *Measuring Globalization. Gauging Its Consequences*. New York: Springer-Verlag, 2008.

Giovanni Federico, Max-Stephan Schulze, and Oliver Volckart, "European goods market integration in the very long run: From the black death to the first world war", *The Journal of Economic History*, 81(1), 2021: 276–308.

Ronald Findlay and Kevin H. O'Rourke, *Power and Plenty: Trade, War, and the World Economy in the Second Millennium*. Princeton: Princeton University Press, 2007.

Richard Florida, "The world is spiky", *The Atlantic Monthly*, October 2005.

Thomas L. Friedman, *The World Is Flat: A Brief History of the Twenty-First Century*. New York: Farrar Straus & Giroux, 2005.

Pankaj Ghemawat, "Why the world isn't flat", *Foreign Policy*, 159, March–April 2007: 54–60.

Samuel P. Huntington, "The clash of civilizations?", *Foreign Affairs*, 72(3), Summer, 1993: 22–49.

Angus Maddison, *The World Economy: A Millennial Perspective/ Historical Statistics: Volume 1: A Millennial Perspective and Volume 2: Historical Statistics: 1–2*. Paris: OECD, 2010.

Peter Miskell, "Entertainment and the film industry", in Teresa da Silva Lopes, Christina Lubinski, and Heidi J.S. Tworek (eds.), *The Routledge Companion to the Makers of Global Business*. London: Routledge, 2019: 377–391.

Maurice Obstfeld and M. Alan Taylor, "Globalization and capital markets", in Michael D. Bordo, Alan M. Taylor, and Jeffrey G. Williamson (eds.), *Globalization in Historical Perspective*. Chicago: The University of Chicago Press, 2003: 121–188.

Dennis O'Flynn and Arturo Giráldez, "Path dependence, time lags and the birth of globalisation: A critique of O'Rourke and Williamson", *European Review of Economic History*, 8(1), 2004: 81–108.

Kevin H. O'Rourke and Jeffrey G. Williamson, "When did globalisation begin?", *European Review of Economic History*, 6(1), 2002: 23–50.

Organization for Economic Co-operation and Development, *OECD Handbook on Economic Globalisation Indicators*. Paris: OECD, various years.

Kevin O'Rourke and Jeffrey G. Williamson, "Late 19th-century Anglo-American factor-price convergence: Were Heckscher and Ohlin Right?", *The Journal of Economic History*, 54(4), 1994: 892–916.

Manfred B. Steger, *Globalization: A Very Short Introduction*. Oxford: Oxford University Press, 2020.

Chapter 4

Inside globalization

DETERMINANTS

IN THE VERY LONG TERM, AS shown in the previous chapters, there have been
several phases of globalization and de-globalization with relevant impacts
on everyday life, on business relationships, and on economic and political
developments at national and international levels. As we have seen, there are
different interpretations of the starting date of the process of globalization, but
there is a general consensus on the fact that globalization has not been linear, but
a "wave-like" process that has experienced accelerations, decelerations, abrupt
halts and reversals of the trend.

The reasons that might explain the waves of globalization and de-globalization
are many and quite complex. This is also explored in depth in Chapters 1 and
7. Each phase has been different and driven by an idiosyncratic mix of factors,
making it therefore impossible to find one single explanatory pattern. However,
there are "common drivers" which, together with other specific factors, have
played a relevant role in fostering or hindering the process of global integration.

While Chapter 7 will provide a more articulated longitudinal and comparative
framework for analyzing the drivers of the integration waves in light of the
current crisis of globalization, this chapter will focus in depth on the three
main determinants that have influenced the global integration trends during
the last two centuries: technology, institutions and culture. These variables
have contributed to create the favorable conditions for a global economy since
the end of the 15th century, and even more during the 19th, 20th and 21st
centuries. On the other hand, they are also behind the reversal of globalization,
for instance in the interwar years.

These determinants fall under the broad category of the so-called "non-
political factors". However, the aim of this book is to introduce readers to the
fact that the realm of politics, both domestic and international, is playing and has
been playing a pivotal role in shaping the conditions under which the processes

   DOI: 10.4324/9780429490255-4

of global integration could take place, both directly and indirectly influencing the non-political determinants described in this chapter. The interaction between political and non-political determinants will be explained more in detail in Chapter 7.

4.1 Technology

Technology and its advances have always played a fundamental role in fostering a global economy since the very early stages of globalization, whichever starting date for globalization is chosen.

Technological developments were a powerful tool to promote globalization for at least two aspects. Firstly, technology transformed humans' capacity to produce goods and services, enormously increasing their amounts and varieties. The emergence of mass production technologies made it necessary to rely on a global community of buyers who were able and willing to consume the new products that technology made it possible to produce. Secondly, and perhaps more importantly in the perspective of this book, technology made it possible to transfer goods, information, people and capital in faster and safer ways.

As discussed in the previous chapters, according to some scholars, globalization started in the late 15th century. The starting point of this phase is conventionally considered to be Columbus' voyages to the Americas, driven by European expansionism and made possible by the advances achieved in maritime navigation technologies a few decades earlier. The caravels in which Columbus and his crew sailed were actually designed in Portuguese shipyards around the mid-15th century. Their lightness and ability to sail fast into the wind made them successful in doing what had been impossible for other ships in the past: crossing the Atlantic Ocean. Old and new technologies like the astrolabe, the magnetic compass and the nocturnal made possible the travels of Ferdinand Magellan, Juan Ponce de León and Amerigo Vespucci in the Age of Exploration.

In a similar fashion, the main drivers of the process of global integration of the 19th century are often said to include the technological improvements made in Europe between the 16th and the 18th centuries and, above all, the achievements of the First and Second Industrial Revolutions, for instance railroads, steamboats and the telegraph, while the main reasons for the Second Global Economy have been indicated as being the Third and, more recently, the Fourth Industrial Revolutions. For example, Industry 4.0 introduced the Global Positioning System, which can provide real-time location-related data on traffic delays, route changes and estimated arrival times, making travel safer and faster.

Each of these technological discontinuities made it at the same time convenient and possible to intensify the flows of people, capital and goods around the world – convenient, since the introduction of the factory system in the late 18th century and the spread of mass production typical of the continuous production processes of the Second Industrial Revolution brought about an unprecedented increase in European and US productive capacity; this in turn implied an additional need for raw materials, export markets and even production facilities situated abroad in several industries.

The main technological discontinuities also made it possible to create a truly global world because, directly or indirectly, they brought devices that incentivized globalization. Technology affected the speed, cost and efficiency of transportation and communications, with remarkable impacts in terms of international flows of people, capital and goods. Thanks to technological innovations in transport and communications, people could travel faster and cheaper. Companies could control and communicate easily with their foreign branches, enlarging their operations. Governments, companies and ordinary people could rapidly obtain information on almost everything, from the political situation in a distant part of the world to the dynamics of the capital markets to price fluctuations to the variety and quality of different raw materials and products, the cost of labor and other critical data.

4.1.1 Ships and cargoes

The 19th-century globalization was largely made possible by a pervasive revolution in the physical transportation of goods and people. The construction of dense railroad networks quickly changed a world in which the maximum speed had depended on humans or animals. The new form of transportation was faster and much more reliable than its predecessors. The transfer of goods and people became considerably cheaper even over long distances. In the two decades between 1850 and 1870, Europe's railroad networks expanded from about 15,000 to 70,000 miles of track. In the US, between 1848 and 1902, the railroad network boomed from 9,495 to 406,359 kilometers of track (Warf, 2008, p. 98). Since punctuality was not dependent on weather conditions or animal energy, the improvement brought by the new form of transport was at least threefold: trains were faster, more punctual and therefore much more reliable. At the same time, steam power was also revolutionizing sea routes. The first steamship for commercial purposes started its voyage in 1807 in Canada's Hudson River. In the second half of the 19th century, large steamships began crossing the oceans; they were faster, more reliable and had more cargo capacity than traditional sail-powered ships. A journey westward from Europe toward the US usually took between three weeks and three months by sailing ship, while by the mid-19th century the same trip could take 10–15 days by steamship. In 1900, the *Kaiser Wilhelm* transatlantic steamship was able to cross the ocean in only five days and seven hours (Warf, 2008, p. 105). Steamships reduced not only shipping time, but also shipping costs: freight rates across the Atlantic dropped by 80 percent between 1815 and 1850, and by another 70 percent between 1870 and 1900 (Pomeranz and Topic, 1999, p. 49).

Technology also made it possible to open up new routes, which completely revolutionized the old transport geography. As described in Chapter 2, the Suez Canal was inaugurated in 1869, cutting the travel distance between London and Bombay by 47 percent. The Panama Canal opened to ships in 1914, cutting 28.968 kilometers off the journey from the Atlantic to the Pacific coasts of the US, saving at least ten days of travel and remarkably reducing costs (Warf, 2008, pp. 108–109).

4.1.2 Telegraph, telephone and radio networks

The telegraph was invented in 1844 and almost immediately adopted for commercial purposes. After improvements and incremental inventions that were pursued according, as far as possible, to homogeneous international standards, a global telegraph system was created in the following decades. Installation of telegraph networks became cheaper and easier during the second part of the 19th century, leading to cheaper and more efficient communication of news over large distances. Thanks to technologically bold initiatives like transoceanic telegraph cables, intercontinental connections soon became reality. While the telegraph efficiently replaced the delivery of short messages delivered by mail, the telephone, invented in 1877, made it for the first time possible to exchange information in a few minutes, or even in a few seconds. Thanks to the telephone, it became possible to transmit 100–200 words per minute rather than the 15–20 per minute words that could be sent in a telegram, although the costs of transoceanic phone calls remained extremely high at least until the 1930s. The impact of this wave of innovations in information and communication technologies was outstanding. For instance, sending information from Great Britain to India took between five and eight months by traditional shipping, six weeks by steamship from the 1840s, a few days by telegraph from the 1850s, and just a few hours after the adoption of the telephone. Finally, thanks to Guglielmo Marconi's invention of the radio, between 1894 and the First World War radio networks were created in many countries, and used to broadcast news and entertainment.

4.1.3 From trucks and automobiles to aircraft and containers

Technological progress steadily improved transport and communications during the interwar years. The gasoline-powered automobile was invented in 1885 by Karl Benz. The first truck using an internal combustion engine was built in 1895. All these means of transportation became mature and common products in the US in the early 20th century and in Europe between the two world wars, making it once again easier and faster for people and goods to travel long distances. Between 1905 and 1940, the number of inhabitants per passenger vehicle dropped from 1,078 to 5 in the US, and from 2,312 to 32 in the UK (Warf, 2008, p. 153).

The 1930s also saw the first prototypes of gas turbines, which would soon make it possible to power supertankers, gigantic container ships and jet airplanes. Fundamental innovations were also developed during the Second World War when governments removed most of the budget constraints to public and private research, enabling – especially in the US and Germany – significant technological achievements in many areas that would foster globalization after the end of the war. These include radar technology, based on the use of electromagnetic waves and already developed during the interwar period, in addition to cabin pressurization, and the jet engine, which had been invented in the 1930s and used in efficient prototypes since the early 1940s.

The wave of innovations known as the Third Industrial Revolution had deep roots in Second World War techniques, and once again revolutionized transport and communication technologies in the decades following the conflict. New materials like aluminum and Plexiglass made it possible to build bigger and faster aircraft, powered by jet engines and using special fuels. The first regularly scheduled jet service connected London to Johannesburg and was established in 1952. The first commercial jet crossed the Atlantic in 1958, prompting a remarkable growth in air traffic for commercial and civil transportation in the following years. The 1950s saw a major innovation in commodity trade come into use: the container. Storage of goods in a container of standard dimensions made transportation dramatically cheaper, prompting a true "container revolution" in the 1960s.

4.1.4 Computer networks and the internet

Simultaneously, computers for non-military use began to spread in the 1950s; the first commercial version of the fax machine was introduced in the mid-1960s, and the first satellite for commercial communications, simultaneously transmitting worldwide voice, data and video, was launched in 1965. The internet, born at the beginning of the 1970s with the interconnection of computer networks, became a tool for commercial activities from the 1990s. The use of personal computers on a global scale from the late 1980s and the technological advancements in both fixed and mobile communications made possible the creation of pervasive global communication networks (see for instance Chandler and Cortada (eds.), 2000).

Once again, in short, in the second half of the 20th century, technology made the various forms of transportation and communications easier, further reducing the cost of trade and simultaneously increasing the volume and circulation of global flows of people, products, capital and information.

Technology made it possible to keep globalization alive, to some extent, even when it was seriously challenged, for instance during the COVID-19 pandemic. What happened during and after the spread of the disease is quite interesting: travel restrictions and the impossibility of meeting in person drove companies and organizations to hold meetings, conferences and a variety of corporate events on online platforms scarcely used beforehand. There was a sudden acceleration in the adoption of internet platforms to support international communication, leading to a remarkable increase in the number, geographic range and frequency of international contacts. Multinationals multiplied meetings involving their subsidiaries even in distant locations, making possible contacts that had previously been much less frequent due to travel costs. Academic conferences, online or in hybrid versions, witnessed the participation of an increasing number of scholars from distant parts of the world who had not been able to attend in person in the pre-pandemic era.

4.2 Institutions

Technological progress is a fundamental prerequisite in processes of global integration; it is necessary, but not sufficient. Institutions, intended as mechanisms of social order that govern the behavior of individuals within a given (national or international) community, play an equally determining role in fostering – and triggering – globalization. As famously stated by Nobel laureate Douglass C. North, institutions can be formal or informal, and deal with every aspect of human life. Among the endless number of arrangements, examples of institutions favoring economic global integration include the adoption of *ad hoc* policies by governments favoring exchanges, international agreements, the homogenization of business practices and of commercial laws and codes, the establishment of standards reducing information asymmetries in different markets, and the implementation of an internationally codified measurement system.

Both qualitative and quantitative studies prove that, together with technological improvements, institutions such as the international monetary system, the existence of trade-enhancing networks (for instance, shared social or ethnic backgrounds that facilitate the transmission of information on market conditions) or trade-enhancing policies created a favorable framework for the First Globalization. Other studies stress the role played by international institutions and free trade agreements in explaining the acceleration of global exchanges during the second part of the 20th century, as well as the impact that both formal (tariffs, transport costs, etc.) and informal (related to cultural and institutional distances) trade barriers between countries had on reducing or even stopping trade. From a more specific business perspective, the reciprocal relationship between governments, as creators of formal institutions, and international companies must be held in great consideration, as a recent work by Neil Rollings, "Government and Regulations" (2019), effectively shows.

This chapter will focus on some social, legal and political institutions that stimulate or trigger the processes of global integration in the long term, and on the role of national governments in this process.

Domestic institutions play a key role in processes of national economic growth and development and therefore play an indirect role in defining global interactions. There is also abundant evidence that institutions have a direct role in stimulating external trade and internationalization of the activities of merchants and companies.

Institutions favorable to economic globalization existed well before the First Industrial Revolution. A good example is the maritime Republic of Venice in the Middle Ages. Venetian merchants crafted institutional "devices" which led to a dramatic improvement in their business activity. One was a specific legal arrangement known as the *consortium*. Existing in many varieties and nuances, this was basically a formal association of several merchants. Each merchant owned a share in the *consortium*. Each share could be different from those of the others. Jointly, the *consortium* purchased a given amount of merchandise to be shipped and traded abroad. The institution of the *consortium* allowed individual merchants to take advantage of scale economies and at the same time to share the risk of dangerous ventures that was a common problem in pre-industrial times. As the expression of the Venetian mercantile elite, the Republic's government designed institutions incentivizing international trade in order to provide centralized coordination and military protection for its mercantile trade over long distances. Although each cargo vessel was in principle free to travel autonomously, this actually never happened. Venetian galleys were gathered into naval caravans (*mude*), each with a specific destination and headed by a captain, who represented the state and was responsible for protecting all the ships in the *muda*. Each *muda* left Venice according to a calendar based on seasonal weather conditions and the commercial cycle of the destination.

Another effective example of pre-industrial institutional arrangements supporting international trade is provided by the privileged companies that operated from the end of the 16th century. These companies operated as monopolies granted by a "charter" that was subject to renewal, in effect a right conceded by a superior authority (the Crown or government) to a body of associated merchants which formed the company, and prohibited anyone else from doing business in the assigned area. These generally had the legal status of joint-stock companies, although local institutions meant that the rules differed in different nations, for instance in the cases of the Dutch and the British East India Companies.

Institutions are key elements for understanding globalization dynamics in the 19th century as well. Some were definitely conducive to industrial growth and were developed increasingly consciously by countries keen to imitate the industrial leaders of the time. This is well exemplified by the case of Japan in the Meiji period, which adopted several institutions that had directly or indirectly favored industrial growth in Western countries during the 18th and 19th centuries and adapted them to local conditions. A good example is the patent system, which aimed to foster innovation by providing protection to intellectual property rights, and would consequently favor the industrialization of the country. Japan's Patent Monopoly Act was designed on the basis of the French Patent Law and was approved in 1885. It was accompanied by the establishment of complementary incentives to patents, such as a large and extensive program of competitive prizes. Competitions were largely financed by local governments and were well attended by the population, favoring the diffusion of advanced technology in the country with huge spillovers for the national industrial system (Nicholas, 2013).

Moreover, the period between 1820 and 1913 was generally characterized by the spread of institutions that gradually removed restrictions on international flows of people, capital and (at least until the 1870s) goods. As anticipated in Chapter 2, during the course of the 19th century restrictions on the movement of people were progressively eliminated both between and within countries. International migration was accepted and, in some cases, incentivized, as in the case of certain countries in North and Latin America. The purpose of attracting immigrants was even part of the constitutional laws in countries that desperately needed a rapid increase in population, such as Argentina.

Control over financial transactions was minimal, and capital could move with no supervision in any direction and in any form, both as foreign direct investment and as portfolio investment, as well as in the form of trade in foreign securities on the stock exchange. People and companies could freely repatriate profits, and in general there was no danger of confiscation for foreign investments abroad although there were no "formal institutions" that officially protected them. An institutional arrangement that undoubtedly supported international flows of capital, reducing – when not eliminating – uncertainty in exchange rates, was the Gold Standard system. This international agreement started in the 1870s and linked the value of a country's currency to its amount of gold reserves, since gold was freely transferable between countries. The Gold Standard led to relatively low inflation, and above all it led to a relatively stable system of exchange rates, with a positive effect on capital flows and on international trade.

Finally, international agreements made the years 1850–1875 the first free-trade era in Europe. The Cobden-Chevalier Treaty signed by Britain and France was the first of a long series of treaties between European nations. Particularly important was the introduction of the "Most Favored Nation" clause, which compelled the signatory nations to extend to the other party any further concessions in terms of lower tariffs that were eventually agreed with a different country. Import prohibitions, quotas and other quantitative restrictions on trade hardly existed before the First World War.

Flows of people, capital and goods were also favored by the fact that the basic political units in this period were the continental and colonial empires. Empires were, of course, very diverse in terms of their internal political structures and institutional organization, but they nonetheless provided a framework in which the mobility of select groups of individuals, goods and finance was relatively free and regulated by the same formal institutions. As mentioned in Chapter 2, most of Phileas Fogg's journey around the world in 80 days took place within the borders of the largest empire on Earth, the British, including former colonies (the US), current colonies, and British possessions in Africa and Asia.

While institutions undoubtedly favored global integration, the crisis of institutional arrangements was one powerful trigger that accelerated de-globalization processes even before the First World War. Except for Britain, the Netherlands and Denmark, a growing majority of countries introduced protectionist tariffs during the last three decades of the 19th century. In the same way, some countries which had previously welcomed large immigration waves, in particular the US and Australia, started to introduce restrictions at the end of the 19th and the beginning of the 20th centuries. Nevertheless, it was the First World War that radically changed the set of written and unwritten norms that characterized the First Global Economy. Nationalism, which had not been non-existent in the previous period, now became a powerful force, impacting on the institutions favoring globalization through the transmission mechanism of domestic politics.

Countries began to impose the use of passports while introducing restrictions in the jobs market. In the US, the 1921 Immigration Act reduced the annual number of legal migrants by two-thirds, down from over 1 million to a maximum of 350,000. It also established that the maximum number of immigrants of any nationality could not exceed 3 percent of the foreign-born population of that nationality resident in the US in 1919. These immigration policies became even more restrictive during the 1920s.

In the absence of institutions explicitly protecting foreign investments and foreign capital abroad, expropriations and confiscations occurred during exceptional events like the First World War and the Soviet Revolution. During the 1920s, a supranational institution, the League of Nations, sought to clarify the obligations of host states toward foreign capital. However, foreign investments were regulated or restricted in many countries, and other expropriations occurred during the interwar years. The most important expropriations in this period took place in Eastern Europe and Latin America, with the Mexican oil industry probably one of the most well-known examples. Multinationals had been welcomed into the country during the 1910s under the regime of Porfirio Díaz. However, after a couple of decades of political turbulence and increasing restrictions in this field, the situation changed completely when Lázaro Cárdenas was elected president in the mid-1930s. When in 1938 the oil multinationals refused to comply with the Mexican Supreme Court decision in support of trade unions demanding higher salaries, Cárdenas decreed the nationalization of all foreign oil properties in the country (Bucheli and Decker, 2021).

The international institution that had favored the flows of capital from one country to another in the previous period, the Gold Standard, was disrupted during and after the First World War, leaving the international monetary system in great disorder. Although many nations returned to the Gold Standard in the mid-1920s, countries both overvalued and undervalued their currencies in relation to gold, thus introducing a further source of instability. The economic crisis of 1929 precipitated the collapse of the international financial and monetary system. The UK abandoned the Gold Standard in 1931, followed by the US and several other nations. Regional currency blocs emerged, each one supported by massive exchange controls.

Policies also became remarkably strict in the field of international trade. After the First World War, protectionism tightened its grip. The Fordney-McCumber Tariff was approved in the US in 1922, raising tariffs to the highest level in the nation's history. Several countries, including Australia, India and some Latin American nations, introduced tariffs together with import quotas and other quantitative restrictions. The League of Nations organized a World Economic Conference in 1927 with a positive, albeit brief, effect on trade relations, which was soon nullified by the Crisis and Great Depression, leading to the collapse of the international trading system. The Smoot-Hawley Act of June 1930 significantly increased general level of US general tariffs, and other countries soon followed this trend, in some cases explicitly adopting autarchic policies.

Supranational and national institutions impacted on dynamics of global integration after the Second World War as well. Domestic institutions did not favor mobility in the decades which followed the conflict, not until the late 1970s. Although several of the world's richest countries began to experience declining birth rates, no relevant openings toward easing migration flows can be detected in this period.

In the aftermath of the Second World War, national policies also aimed to regulate, and often to restrict, international flows of capital, with a direct impact on the overall level of foreign direct investments. The situation was worsened by the fact that the Communist bloc was only marginally affected by international flows of capital in the form of direct investments, while former colonies, now independent countries, often treated foreign investments with suspicion and hostility, particularly in the case of former colonizers. Foreign investments were also restricted within the capitalist bloc, where entire sectors were excluded by law from direct foreign influence. Some countries even discouraged multinational investments, at least in the form of wholly owned subsidiaries. In the first two decades of Francisco Franco's dictatorship in Spain, for instance, the newly established regime decided to promote an autarchic development plan. The country was industrially backward and needed foreign capital, technologies and know-how. At the same time, however, the Spanish government wanted to promote national business and protect it from foreign competition. The state undertook a variety of actions in order to discourage the autonomous entry of foreign investments. For example, non-residents were not allowed to convert the peseta to other currencies, and the Francoist administration had the power to arbitrarily allow or deny the authorization of new investments. Moreover, Spanish legislation did not permit foreigners to hold majority shares of the capital of a Spanish corporation.

The political and legal environment in Spain became much more open to foreign investments from the late 1950s onward, but many other countries continued systematic discouragement of foreign investments in the following decades, both emerging and industrialized nations, as in the case of Japan. Japanese policy became extremely restrictive in the early 1930s, and this continued after the Second World War. Foreign direct investments were again permitted only after 1949, but new investments required government approval; the Foreign Investment Law of 1950 established that each foreign investment proposal had to be screened and approved. Foreign investors were usually pressured to abandon the country and license their technology to a local firm or establish a joint venture with a local partner. Liberalization began only in the late 1960s, with sectors unlikely to receive foreign investments, such as soy sauce. Entirely foreign ownership was allowed only in some industries, while the foreign share was limited to 50 percent in others. The Foreign Investment Law was abolished in 1980, but restrictions remained in specific sectors like agriculture and financial services.

Flows of capital were regulated by exchange controls in order to avoid impact on the balance of payments, in order to ensure the stability of the system of fixed exchange rates introduced at Bretton Woods, under the supervision of two supranational institutions established at the end of the Second World War: the International Monetary Fund and the World Bank. It was only after the gradual dismantlement of the fixed exchange rates from the early 1970s that a remarkable increase in the flows of capital became possible again in the following decades.

However, it was the widespread adoption of policies inspired by the "Washington Consensus" that turned deregulation in international financial markets into a common credo, while privatizations and liberalizations opened up new market opportunities for foreign investors. Several governments began to adopt policies aimed at attracting foreign firms, although these policies differed radically among different countries; some nations explicitly allowed the intervention of foreign capital and investors as key players in their respective privatization programs. While only in a very few cases did governments explicitly oppose the activity of foreign investors, investment was frequently subject to certain conditions, for instance the compulsory involvement of a local partner. Both foreign direct investment and portfolio investments began to flow massively into emerging markets, with restrictions generally applied only to certain industries.

Government intervention during the second half of the 20th century and at the start of the new millennium, however, was not limited only to the regulation of inward flows of foreign capital and investment. Governments were also active agents in promoting rules and institutions that encouraged local companies to internationalize. Examples of this can be found in Japan's coordinated internationalization policy of the 1970s and 1980s, or in the aggressive investment policies of Chinese state-owned enterprises today, with internationalization actively incentivized by the government.

National and international institutions and policies adopted by governments proved crucial in supporting international trade following the Second World War as well. The General Agreement on Tariffs and Trade (1947) represented an important step toward lowering trade barriers and creating a positive environment for international trade, and this trend increased during the following decade. The institution of supranational trading blocs like the European Economic Community (1957) fueled international exchanges, while the worldwide adoption of policies inspired by the Washington Consensus implied a general reduction of tariffs and non-tariff barriers in both developed and developing countries. This was particularly the case from the late 1980s onward, although several countries, including India and China, still adopted protectionist policies, and international trade in many commodities was still distorted by subsidies and tariffs.

4.3 Culture

An additional determinant of globalization and de-globalization processes falls into the category of cultural attitudes, in its turn directly influencing the dynamics of institution-building. Different attitudes, both toward globalization as a whole and toward the acceptance of foreign influence of any kind, had alternating fortunes over time. Between the two extreme attitudes of *globaphilia* (extolling the positive aspects of globalization, including the positive impacts on economic growth and the spread of democracy as the most efficient political regime), and *globaphobia* (emphasizing the negative impacts of globalization in terms of rising inequality levels and exploitation of marginal societies) there are infinite nuances.

Investigations of the nature of a "global culture" flourished, especially from the early 1990s onward, although there was no lack of critics of "cultural imperialism" during the 1970s and 1980s. While the concept of *cultural differentialism* is that cultures tend to remain determinedly different one from another, a distinct theoretical approach emphasizes the emergence of a "global culture", based on a set of transnational paradigms in a variety of different fields – politics, business, education, family, religion and so on – and that their spread has dramatically increased the level of uniformity across the world. The concept of *cultural hybridization* is that of cultural mixing and combination as a result of globalization, leading to the emergence of new and unique hybrid cultures that are neither local nor purely global cultures. The concept of *cultural convergence* is that globalization tends to foster homogenization. Furthermore, the concept of *cultural imperialism* is the imposition of one or more cultures on others in a process that can be more or less conscious, but which destroys local specificities. More explicitly, some scholars have proposed the term *grobalization* to label the imperialistic ambitions of nation-states, corporations and organizations trying to impose themselves on the global scenario. Whatever its definition and origins, it is certain that globalization needs to be culturally grounded in a framework of more or less conscious acceptance of its outcomes.

World historian Erik Ringmar argued that standard economy-based explanations should be complemented with explanations of a cultural nature, taking as an example the case of European expansionism versus Chinese isolationism in the early modern period. He used the case of three giraffes — gifted to local rulers and received in different cultural environments and attitudes — to show how diverse cultures saw the exotic and how cultural predisposition might have favored foreign explorations or closure (Ringmar, 2006).

The first of the giraffes appeared in Florence under Lorenzo De Medici in 1486, as a gift from the Mamluk sultan of Egypt. In the cultural framework of "outward-looking curiosity" that characterized the Renaissance, Florentines seeing the giraffe could probably begin to imagine exotic worlds and their entertainment potential and develop a desire to explore them. The giraffe strolled about the streets, acclaimed by poets like Angelo Poliziano, and immortalized in many paintings. In the following decades, Florence was home to several explorers, of whom the most famous is probably Amerigo Vespucci; in 1497, just a few years after the arrival of the giraffe, Vespucci set sail for the Americas. The economic aim of many explorations became that of satisfying a booming European market in exotic goods.

The second giraffe was presented to the Chinese Emperor in Beijing in 1414 as a gift from the ruler of Bengal. In a culture oriented toward "inward-looking self-sufficiency", Confucian scholars stated that it must be a unicorn. The arrival of this mythological creature was regarded as proof of the emperor's virtue. A couple of decades later, a series of decrees severely restricted overseas travel and trade by Chinese subjects. The self-confidence of the Celestial Empire remained extremely high in the following centuries, and in 1793 the emperor Qianlong still claimed that China had not the slightest need for goods manufactured in other countries.

The third giraffe appeared in Paris in 1827 as a gift from the ruler of Egypt. The influence of the Enlightenment's cultural "outward-looking self-sufficiency" led the French to classify the animal as a *Giraffa camelopardis*. The "French" giraffe occupied a ready-made slot in the great universal taxonomy designed for it, demonstrating that the animal kingdom was subjected to the laws established by scientific investigation and that Europeans possessed intellectual superiority over the rest of the world, knowing more about Egypt and Africa than the Egyptians and Africans themselves. People's spontaneous curiosity was commercially driven, and the giraffe became a consumer "product" in the form of textiles, wallpapers, soaps and furniture. However, the French soon lost interest in the giraffe and moved on. Three years later, France's first imperialist venture in Africa began.

This – and other examples – help show how culture was a powerful determinant driving Europeans abroad to explore the "unknown" world, leading to the proto-globalization wave of the 16th century. At the same time, Europeans found acceptance abroad, not only due to their weapons, technology and stronger health immunities, but also because what they brought with them in cultural terms was accepted by local people and elites.

Positive attitudes toward foreign products and cultures can help explain the incentives for international merchants of the Middle Ages who invested in the trade in spices and other exotic items transported to Europe. Trading activities became more extensive over time, including an increasing range of goods. Together with the products traded, cultural features were also involved in the exchange. China's insatiable thirst for silver made it convenient for European merchants to establish a regular transport service from the Americas (the Manila Galleons) across the vast Pacific Ocean. In turn, China expanded its production of silk and porcelain directed at European markets. Profits from international activities had a positive impact on living standards in Western Europe. This in turn led to increased consumption of Indian cotton and the greater availability and range of exotic products on offer in Europe. Among the various signs of cross-cultural contacts and influence, it is possible to mention the impact of European painting styles among the upper classes in India, as well as the name Mary given to many Indian girls. The Japanese upper-class and civil servants began to dress in European-style clothing, and Europeans enjoyed high esteem in China for their knowledge of clock-making, while European imports included exotic animals and curative plants from the Far East (Stearns, 2020).

However, these new contacts were not easy. Europeans were proud of their accomplishments in arts and technology and approached the rest of the world with an attitude of superiority. The fear of uncontrolled destabilization of consolidated power structures often made foreign influence and culture something to keep at bay.

By the end of the 16th century, and after Spain had conquered the Philippines, Japanese leaders became increasingly suspicious of the potential impact of Spanish influence on Japanese culture, fearing that the country's consolidated feudal social and political order could be destroyed by uncontrolled access to European military technologies. As a result, they precipitated their country into isolation for approximately two centuries. Similarly, after a long phase of "benign neglect", Chinese rulers became hostile to Western culture, and their zealous desire to preserve the cultural and social order from outside influence found a target of repression in the Christian missionaries. Ottoman authorities also held Western influence at bay; the press was not permitted in the Empire until the 1730s in order to preserve political control over public opinion. Thus, cultural exchanges were artificially and consciously limited in several cases, via more or less effective strategies of isolation.

Cultural attitudes toward integration began to change again during the 19th century, when the sudden acceleration in the volume of international trade and business was openly supported by a positive cultural attitude that favored the First Globalization as an ultimately positive force. Examples of reciprocal cultural influence and of acceptance of different cultures can be found in several different fields and in very distant parts of the globe.

Many European artists, of whom Vincent Van Gogh is one of the most famous, took their inspiration from African and Japanese art in the late 19th century, and even before the turn of the century there is plenty of evidence of artists from Latin America and the US who came to Europe to train in the new styles. Driven by the personal desire to find a new dimension in his life, Paul Gauguin left Paris for French Polynesia, flooding the Paris art market with his exotic portraits of Tahitian teenagers. Scientific societies began to sponsor study missions to centers of science and technology in Western Europe and in the US. In post-Meiji Restoration Japan, study missions like the famous Iwakura Mission took dozens of young Japanese students around the world and were instrumental in accelerating the country's modernization process; China did the same in its desperate bid to catch up with the West.

The most brilliant pupils of indigenous colonial elites began to be educated in the so-called "motherland", as in the famous case of Mahatma Gandhi. Even inside the advanced West, "study tours" took place, allowing the circulation not only of technical knowledge, but also of different cultural experiences. For example, the young Italian graduate Giovanni Battista Pirelli undertook a highly formative tour of Europe to explore new business opportunities.

As mentioned in Chapter 2, globalization was also built via the construction of a vision of the world as being in "common" for all mankind. For Westerners, remote regions of the globe were still unknown and worth exploring: the North-west Passage, for instance, was successfully navigated between 1903 and 1906 by Amundsen, who sailed from Greenland to Alaska. Africa was the main target for Victorian explorers like the legendary David Livingstone, while geographers traveled into Central Asia's unknown territories in order to measure the Himalayan peaks (and push the borders of the British Raj even further north).

In addition, as mentioned in previous chapters, globalization had an impact on popular culture, both in terms of consumption and leisure. Western-inspired department stores opened in a number of the major cities of several nations, including Russia, Japan and China, while Western clothing styles began to compete with local fashions. Other specific products such as tooth powder became increasingly common around the world, while sports began to globalize from the late 19th century. The modern Olympic Games, launched in 1896, were founded on the ideal that sports were a driver of cosmopolitan harmony. The popularity of American baseball and British football (soccer) began spreading from their original homelands to reach a global audience and an endless number of players. Starting in the early 20th century, the movie industry became an important driver for the creation of a global culture, contributing to a first wave of "Americanization". The Paris *Exposition Universelle* in 1900 was an iconic celebration of the world's new global identity that had developed after the end of the Napoleonic Wars. During the seven months it was open, nearly 50 million tourists visited the *Exposition*'s pavilions, whose contents allowed them to "travel" around the world.

The tomb of the First Globalization, the First World War, represented a radical discontinuity with the past also in terms of mutual acceptance of different cultures. As Chapter 7 will analyze in depth, cosmopolitan attitudes were thwarted by nationalistic impulses that would become bolder during the interwar years. Global cosmopolitanism was blamed as a force corrupting local societies, although the internationalization of movies, sports and other leisure activities persisted, and cosmopolitan experiences remained a fundamental part of the education of the elites in some countries well after the conflict. It was in the 1920s, for instance, that many US universities first established regular foreign study programs, believing that, even in a framework of increasing nationalism, exposure to cosmopolitan experience should be a fundamental component of higher education. Cultural influences from outside were strictly limited by Soviet leaders, while Japan and Germany started processes of economic decoupling between the late 1920s and the early 1930s in order to reduce their dependence on the world economy. In an attempt to rejuvenate Germany's native culture, the Nazi regime famously banned modern "degenerate" cosmopolitan art. In this cultural climate, it is little surprise that international companies adopted "camouflage" strategies, hiding their original names and changing their products' branding in order to appear "local" rather than "international".

The decades which followed the Second World War were quite contradictory in terms of cultural acceptance of globalization. While the Soviet Union continued to pursue a policy of economic, political and cultural isolation from the global system, the process of decolonization reinforced the emergence of national identities and cultures, often ideologically rejecting the cultural influences of former colonizers.

The overwhelming influence of the Western world – and particularly of the US in this period – became a source of concern in several countries, while in others it was an outstanding success. In Europe, American companies enjoyed enormous market opportunities thanks to an ongoing process of cultural homogenization known as the "Americanization" of European identity. The US supported this process in a wide variety of ways, including soft control over executives' education and the internationalization of consulting companies that spread codes of US-made "best practices" across the globe (see for instance Kipping, 1999). The diffusion of English as a global standard language was at first due to the need for easier communication in a new phase of globalization. However, the common language soon also enabled the creation of other favorable conditions for globalization.

Cultural movements spread worldwide from the US and, to a lesser extent, from Western Europe, starting from the 1950s. This disproportionate Western influence has begun to weaken only since the last decades of the 20th century. Japan, and subsequently also China, Brazil, India and many other countries, became dominant centers for cultural elaboration between the last decades of the 20th century and the early decades of the new millennium, while global culture moved from an overwhelming Western influence in several new directions. For instance, a US citizen may listen to European music, play Japanese video games, look to Chinese medicine and watch Bollywood Indian movies. Globalization has involved multiple cultural fields in the last decades, creating an international public for sports, games, food and beverages, fashion, and even religious events, with the commercial aspects of Christmas being widespread even in non-Christian countries.

The spread of social media and networks has accelerated particularly since the beginning of the new millennium. This has contributed to the transformation of global culture from a "one-way" phenomenon fueled by television, movies and newspapers into something far more interactive. Social media allow people to create, share and exchange information and ideas in virtual communities and networks, making it possible for an increasing number of users to be immediately and simultaneously in touch with events elsewhere in the world. The capillary diffusion of smartphones has incremented this process by making the internet available even to low-income populations.

The creation of a global culture has been one of the most evident aspects of globalization waves. This has, in the course of time, offered enormous business opportunities for globally active companies, which are themselves also true agents of globalization. The next chapter will examine the relationship between international business and globalization.

References

Marcelo Bucheli and Stephanie Decker, "Expropriation of foreign property and political alliances: A business historical approach". *Enterprise and Society*, 22(1), 2021: 247–284.

Alfred D. Chandler, Jr. and James W. Cortada (eds.), *A Nation Transformed by Information How Information Has Shaped the United States from Colonial Times to the Present*. New York: Oxford University Press, 2000.

Matthias Kipping, "American Management Consulting Companies in Western Europe, 1920 to 1990: Products, Reputation and Relationships", *The Business History Review*, 73(2), 1999: 190–220.

Tom Nicholas, "Hybrid innovation in Meiji Japan", *International Economic Review*, 52(2), 2013: 575–600.

Kenneth Pomeranz and Steven Topik, *The World That Trade Created. Society, Culture, and the World Economy, 1400-the Present*. New York: M.E. Shape, 1999.

Erik Ringmar, "Audience for a giraffe: European expansionism and the quest for exotic", *Journal of World History*, 17(4), 2006: 375–398.

Neill Rollings, "Government and regulators", in Teresa da Silva Lopes, Christina Lubinski, and Heidi J. S. Tworek (eds.), *The Routledge Companion to the Makers of Global Business*. London: Routledge, 2019: 95–108.

Peter N. Stearns, *Globalization in World History*. New York: Routledge, 2020.

Barney Warf, *Time-Space Compression: Historical Geographies*. New York: Routledge, 2008.

Chapter 5

Globalization and business

5.1 Globalization and international business

Chapter 4 ended by mentioning the biunivocal relationship between globalization and business. Internationally active companies mostly benefited from the favorable framework created by the positive interaction between technological progress (goods and raw materials traveled across borders thanks to innovations in transportation and infrastructural progress), institutions (which positively impacted on the cost of trade and on the uncertainty surrounding exchanges) and cultural attitudes (which created a friendly environment for foreign companies and their products). In turn, companies and entrepreneurial activities must be considered the true engines of the technological advancements that, as seen in Chapter 4, were among the main determinants of globalization (see for instance Jones, 2005; Fitzgerald, 2016; Da Silva et al., 2019). At the same time, companies and entrepreneurs continually attempted to influence decision-makers to design policies favorable to their interests, while actively supporting the spread of consumer behavior toward global consumption styles.

Historically speaking, the proto-globalization that began in the 15th century was heavily based on the initiatives of merchants, merchant guilds, chartered companies, and subsequently on trading and manufacturing companies. These all contributed to the creation of basic trade infrastructures, building larger and more resistant ships and advancing navigation techniques, as well as introducing exotic items into their domestic markets while exporting domestic goods abroad. They were also active in seeking and obtaining support from their own governments to obtain protection in situations of risk. The interconnecting webs of communication and information during the First Globalization, from submarine cables to steamships and railroads, were built by private companies, as during the current integration wave, relying on complex public-private partnerships in transportation and communication services. In both of the last

 DOI: 10.4324/9780429490255-5

two globalization waves, moreover, companies actively created new markets for specific products; for example, German electrical manufacturers at the turn of the 20th century invested heavily in the establishment of electric energy systems abroad with the collateral aim of opening overseas markets for the electrical equipment they produced.

In the mean time, entrepreneurs traveled abroad to learn and also to spread knowledge, thus favoring the globalization of competences. To a greater or lesser degree, some businesses lobbied their governments to facilitate their global expansion, while others even demanded government protection from foreign competition. At the same time, when companies crossed borders they brought with them knowledge, cultures and consumption models that spread into foreign countries and contributed to the strengthening of a common global set of shared tangibles and intangibles. In short, as true agents of globalization, business companies played a pivotal role in shaping the intensity and the effectiveness of the main determinants of globalization.

Globalization waves were not at all neutral as far as business enterprise is concerned. Processes of market integration posed a serious threat to companies and entire industries when they were suddenly challenged by what were often unexpected competitive forces from outside the domestic market. In some cases, this had (and still has) positive effects in terms of competitive stimuli, but in others it meant corporate decline and failure for entire industries. This is well exemplified by the divergent experiences of a furniture and a maritime cluster in the same region on Norway's west coast. Both emerged at the beginning of the 20th century, but their experiences when global competition increased at the end of the century were completely different. The furniture cluster had never needed to satisfy a strong group of demanding customers, and did not develop distinctive competencies; it was unable to deal with global competition and went into decline when the industry began to establish production largely abroad, decoupling the location of production from the market. On the other hand, the maritime cluster comprised close interactions between the local suppliers of equipment yards, supporting institutions and highly demanding customers who needed high-quality vessels, especially for deep-sea fishing fleets and later on for offshore operations; this enabled the development of advanced and distinctive skills. When this cluster encountered globalization at the end of the 20th century, it was extremely successful in satisfying highly demanding foreign customers and attracting foreign direct investment (FDI) in local competences (Amdam and Bjarnar, 2015).

Overall, globalization undoubtedly represented a shock. The immediate reaction was often to appeal for government protection at home, while in the medium to long term, positive aspects prevailed for competitive enterprises because they had access to global markets, technologies and cheap or even specialized labor forces. New companies emerged during the globalization waves, and integration also played an important role in modeling the strategies and structures of both existing and new firms, whether they remained active on a local scale or decided to operate at an international level.

The diffusion and strengthening of international mercantile ventures, followed by the emergence of the multinational enterprise during the 19th century, is of course closely linked with globalization and its determinants. This was the outcome of favorable institutional conditions, such as the constant diffusion of free trade and reduction of barriers to capital transfers and foreign investments, accompanied by the presence of empires across many parts of the world. In turn, favorable institutional and political conditions were accompanied by a widespread cultural propensity toward foreign products and consumption models, which were easily, cheaply and effectively transferred using the new technologies.

This chapter will focus on the multiple impacts that globalization waves had on business activities in the long term, while also focusing on the progressive emergence of new models of companies that were internationally active during phases of globalization and de-globalization.

5.2 Pre-industrial global business

International business was a standard practice well before the emergence of modern multinational companies in the last decades of the 19th century. As anticipated in the previous chapters, merchants and companies were doing business internationally well before the beginning of the industrial era. Of course, pre-industrial international business was largely focused on trading and only marginally involved FDI.

This was the case of international merchants in the Middle Ages, who progressively extended the range of their long-distance activities. At the end of the 15th century, international trade networks, which were generally managed by guild members (Casson, 2019), had enlarged considerably, particularly on the Eurasian continent. At the same time, international merchants had developed sophisticated strategies to reduce extremely high transaction costs and to cope with uncertainty and risk, such as adopting product and geographic diversification strategies, creating partnerships to share risks, or establishing a mutual defense force to travel on commercial ships and protect merchants from piracy. It was, however, rare that the trading activities of individual merchants gave origin to stable bureaucratic organizations that outlived their founders. The cost of internalizing transactions was relatively high; in order to reduce risks, individual merchants would diversify their range of activities in terms of the goods they traded and the geographic area covered. They would also deal simultaneously with several transactions in different locations, which dramatically reduced any incentive to internalize transactions in a single stable organization.

The explorations and discoveries that began in the second part of the 15th century, and the process of European colonization over the following centuries, radically transformed the nature of international business and the features of the business actors involved. If the presence of multiple, stable and long-distance trade relationships is defined as a "trade cluster", during the 16th and 17th centuries there were at least three such clusters. The oldest one included the Eurasian trade relationships occurring roughly across the ancient Silk Road, while the Atlantic cluster began to emerge and consolidate after Columbus' voyages to the Americas, and the Pacific cluster appeared after 1571, when the Spanish Crown seized Manila to achieve dominance in the Pacific. The first cluster developed from the merger of two existing trade systems: the European system (including the Baltic, North Sea and Mediterranean sub-trade systems) and the Asian. During the Middle Ages, the Eurasian trade was based on an articulated system of land routes that were largely substituted by alternative sea routes when the *Pax Mongolica* disintegrated in the mid-14th century. China's silk, spices, tea and porcelain, India's fabrics, spices and semi-precious stones, Europe's woolen goods and furs, and Arab horses are only a few of the numerous products that typically traveled these routes. The Atlantic cluster consolidated from the 16th century with European exploration of the Americas, linking the New World to Europe's Atlantic coast. In the initial stage, Spain and Portugal were the main players, importing precious metals and natural resources from Central and South America, and subsequently exporting some of these, especially silver, to Asia. Nonetheless, the huge opportunities provided by this cluster of trading routes soon attracted the interest of other Western Europeans, like the British, Dutch and French, who were progressively involved in the growing activities of trading natural resources from the Americas, manufactured goods from Europe and slaves from Africa. The Pacific trade cluster became consolidated from the last three decades of the 16th century and was at first managed mainly by the Spanish and Portuguese; their center of activities was based in Southeast Asia, and they became the main players in the intra-Asian and American-Asian trade. The Spanish "Silver Galleons", or "Manila Galleons", transported enormous quantities of precious metals from the Americas to China, which needed them to sustain its taxation system based entirely on silver, and then transported exotic merchandise back to Acapulco. By the mid-17th century, the three intercontinental trade systems had become consolidated.

This new framework offered remarkable opportunities to merchants, who were encouraged by the considerable increase in the volume of international trade. However, the framework for international business was very different from that in which individual medieval merchants had operated, for instance, in the Mediterranean area. Navigation-related risks became significantly higher, since sailing on the open ocean was much more difficult and dangerous than previous sea travel. Transaction costs soared, since merchants now dealt directly with different cultures, needed to acquire familiarity with different languages, religions and habits, and encountered previously unknown units of measurement. The duration of business travel increased with the size of cargo ships and their crews; this had an obvious impact on the size of fixed and variable costs, and therefore on capital expenditure, not to mention the deferred return on each investment. The new conditions put great pressure on the pre-existent structure of international trade, as described above, based as it was on individual merchants and their associates, but ultimately acting through other merchants as intermediaries on the basis of personal contacts or family ties; this old system became increasingly inefficient. A new kind of firm, usually a "chartered" or "privileged company", soon established itself as the main protagonist of long-distance trade. These new organizations based their success on the ability to reduce the transaction costs involved in the increasing volume of long-distance international trade.

5.3 Privileged chartered companies

Chartered companies have sometimes been defined as precursors of modern multinationals. These new organizational structures emerged in the late 16th century as the major players in international business, capable of trading consistent quantities of items and goods. Although they differed greatly from one another in terms of their aims, size, organizational form and geographic area, all shared some common features (Colli, 2016). The first of these is their duration: while partnerships of individual merchants normally lasted no more than several years, sometimes just for the duration of a single business trip, chartered companies were created to survive their founders and to conduct a stable business activity in the long term. The Dutch East India Company, for instance, was active over two centuries; the British East India Company, established in 1600, was officially dissolved in 1874.

A second common feature is that these companies operated as monopolies, since the "charter" granted by the highest state authority gave them the right to trade in a specific geographical area and/or regarding specific kinds of merchandise under a monopoly regime. The rationale behind this concession was government interest in having national companies involved in foreign activities; from a mercantilist perspective, the repatriation of profits would increase the home nation's domestic wealth. The perspective of political economy was also an important factor, since the chartered companies, although formed with private capital, were also powerful tools of colonial penetration into distant areas of the world. The granting of a charter gave a powerful incentive to domestic companies to venture into risk-intensive long-distance trade, since the status conferred by the charter allowed a firm to operate in a relatively "safe" environment, at least with regard to market competition.

The third common feature was that these firms enjoyed the support of their respective governments, which encouraged them to pursue mercantilist aims and to strengthen their international political influence. Some companies were allowed to maintain a kind of private army, and the home government would "outsource" its sovereignty to a company in a specific geographical area of influence. The strong relationship between long-distance trade activities, political power and chartered companies is well exemplified in the case of Britain. The presidents of the British East India Company were considered perfect substitutes for British colonial governors.

A fourth common feature is that each company had its specific geographical focus. The area that each company dealt with differed in each case. For some companies, this was quite narrowly focused; the Barbary Company, for example, dealt only with Morocco. Other companies had much wider ranges; the Dutch India Company controlled trade between the Dutch Provinces of Holland and Zeeland and also across a vast area of the Pacific Ocean between the Cape of Good Hope and the Straits of Magellan. Many of these companies were created to exchange domestically produced goods for colonial natural resources, while others exploited and transferred natural resources from one part of the world to another. The British Royal African Company was originally established to exploit the gold mines of what is now Gambia, but soon diversified its activities and took a leading role in the slave trade from Africa to the Americas.

A fifth common feature of chartered companies stems directly from their need to raise enormous amounts of capital to invest in their long-distance trade, and thus their legal status. Privileged companies were stable associations of merchants, some with hundreds of stockholders. At its foundation, the British East India Company counted 219 members. The Dutch East India Company was a joint-stock company which at the outset gave all its stockholders the right to withdraw their capital at the end of each decade. This was, however, soon modified to favor the stability of the firm, so that stockholders could no longer simply withdraw their capital, but were instead compelled to sell their shares to another stockholder. As a result, within a few decades the firm's ownership had become extremely dispersed.

The sixth shared feature of these companies is their commitment to invest in the ownership of stable facilities abroad. Although the type and size of investment varied greatly, it was common for companies to invest in military installations or in operational facilities like yards, warehouses and factories for the collection, storage and preparation for delivery of traded goods. Chartered companies also invested in ships, which they owned directly, and in some cases also in shipyards. Sometimes they invested in production, often in response to a series of pressures such as the need to ensure a stable flow of goods to the mother country or to control the quality of the products they traded.

Finally, the chartered companies were established to handle a significantly high volume of trade in a complex environment, and this made them pioneers in the adoption of sophisticated organizations with large workforces. The Dutch East India Company was not only the Netherlands' largest employer, but also employed workers abroad. In 1625, the company had around 5,000 people (including sailors, seamen, soldiers, administrative personnel, workers, churchmen, servants) located abroad, and by the end of the 18th century this had risen to 25,000. The fact that chartered companies dealt with a large volume of transactions across distant markets made it convenient for them to internalize transactions and obliged them to face new challenges in terms of internal organization. They needed mechanisms to collect, process and refine the mass of information generated by the sheer volume of their trading activities involving different markets and products. Most chartered companies adopted a similar form of organization. They were generally headed by a board of directors, the "Court", located in the country of incorporation and formed by the main shareholders; this body was often closely connected with the government and was responsible for taking the most important central strategic decisions. The Court was supported by committees made up of salaried managers, whose functional responsibilities would typically include accounting, shipping and procurement. The parts of the organization located abroad could be very complex. In the most sophisticated companies, the area covered by the charter was divided into foreign trading areas under the responsibility of a local council. In turn, these local councils were connected to the managers of the local factories or trading posts where most of the basic exchanges took place. There was a strong emphasis on standardization, and the largest companies typically elaborated standard procedures for all routine activities. In this framework, the managers were effectively company servants, and firms began to look for ways of bringing agency costs under control.

The role of chartered companies did not end the activity of international merchants. In some cases, the latter's long-distance trade simply took place over routes or through businesses not under chartered control. Some merchants remained active in an independent position, although sometimes subordinate to charter companies. Others concealed their activities behind their roles as servants of privileged companies. For others, in cases when the charter was simply a device that made individual trading over long distances easier and the charter company was essentially an umbrella organization of individual merchants, the situation did not actually change greatly.

The growth of international trade and the rise of this new form of international company was accompanied by the transformation of local companies in the home and host countries, as they adapted to the new opportunities and challenges generated by the high volume of operations and long-distance trade of these huge international players.

5.4 The First Globalization: from international traders to multinationals

Until the 19th century, despite the high level of organizational sophistication achieved by these large corporations, they had to rely on weak transport and communication systems in a very risky and unpredictable external environment; this made it extremely difficult for them to develop efficient management and coordination systems. The situation changed dramatically with the First Industrial Revolution; from the end of the 18th century, the nature of capitalism was transformed as the "industrial" component was added to the "merchant" component, thereby paving the way for a real revolution in transport and communication systems.

In its early stage, the astonishing increase in productivity due to the introduction of machinery and the new inanimate sources of energy into factories affected the nature of international trade, driving the increasing demand for raw materials, semi-finished inputs and finished goods.

Chartered companies were doomed. Some had already ceased to exist for various reasons even before the start of industrialization. Many had lost their privileges under pressure from the increasing volumes of trade and the growing criticism of their monopolistic activities. The decline of chartered companies was accompanied by the rise of trading companies. British merchants and traders dominated the first three-quarters of the 19th century, also because Britain, the first industrial country, became a hub for imports of the raw materials required for industrial production of manufactured goods. British merchant houses and trading firms, which were originally individual entrepreneurial ventures located abroad in the main industrial areas and promising markets, operated in what was almost a standard way. In a first stage of activity, they imported goods (mainly cotton textiles) from Britain and exported local merchandise as they accumulated know-how and contacts. In a second stage, they diversified their activities through a process of vertical integration into shipping and/or production, or else via horizontal expansion into quasi-related businesses, mainly banking services. As the process of industrialization and globalization consolidated, business occasions also emerged for other industrializing countries, which also found their vocation in foreign markets.

Industrialization and globalization also accompanied migration, which included entrepreneurs. Many of those who had some technological knowledge or market skills took advantage of opportunities abroad, migrating to foreign countries to start business ventures. A good example of this is the investments of Swiss cotton entrepreneurs in Italy before Unification in 1861. In many cases, emigration was not permanent and the contacts with Switzerland persisted in the form of share ownership. In some cases, the decision to invest abroad involved the replication of managerial competences that had been developed in the countries of origin, anticipating the model of the multinational enterprise that would become pervasive just a few decades later.

While the early impact of industrialization on business mainly involved trading, as the globalization process became more intensive and transportation and communication costs decreased with increasing efficiency, cross-border investments accelerated. From the end of the Napoleonic Wars, some companies started to make cross-border investments without the protection of monopolistic rights. From the 1830s, British merchants and bankers established "overseas" banks in Australia, Canada and the West Indies colonies. Around the mid-19th century, entrepreneurs started to open factories abroad, which they managed from their home countries. The German Siemens and the US Singer Sewing Machines both established foreign plants during the 1850s and 1860s, and are considered to be among the first modern multinationals; from the 1870s onward, multinational firms steadily increased in number, size and range of activity (Jones, 2005).

The acceleration in cross-border investment led to the emergence of a variety of forms of international enterprise. Alongside individual entrepreneurs, hundreds of "free-standing companies" now appeared: firms incorporated in one country with the purpose of doing business abroad, but without any prior domestic business. According to some estimates, by 1914 these companies accounted for approximately 40 percent of the total stock of foreign investments from European countries; these were led by Britain, but also included Belgium, the Netherlands and France. Others involved were Japan, the US, Canada, Australia, New Zealand and South Africa. Free-standing companies were typically established in developed countries, whose companies had developed sophisticated know-how, but where opportunities for domestic growth were limited. They invested predominantly in the development of "peripheries" with abundant natural resources (like gutta-percha for submarine telegraph cables, tea, coffee and palm plantations, and minerals) and/or which needed transport infrastructure (such as urban tramways) and utilities (such as electricity, water production and distribution networks), whose construction required advanced technical knowledge and large amounts of capital. Free-standing companies therefore acted as powerful connectors, and were efficient vehicles for the transfer of financial capital and technical competences.

Despite the improvements in transportation and communications, both "migrant" entrepreneurs and free-standing firms faced high coordination and integration costs. This meant that they mostly employed relatives, friends and fellow citizens in order to reduce control and agency costs, while a relatively "loose" relationship prevailed between parent companies and their subsidiaries.

However, this changed radically during the last decades of the 19th century, when the Second Industrial Revolution profoundly transformed the nature of the large business enterprise. This was mainly the consequence of applied scientific research. On the one hand, it made a cluster of new products available, especially new process technologies based on chemicals and mostly involving transformation of raw materials: steel production, oil refinery and almost all branches of the chemical industry. This also meant widespread production of standardized parts for assembly into complex products like sewing machines, watches, machine tools or cars. The industries that applied these new production techniques began to enjoy economies of scale and scope to an extent never previously experienced, and this drove companies to build gigantic production plants.

These giant corporations needed large amounts of capital and energy, and relied on the impressive developments in communications and transport that made both goods delivery and information transfer easier, faster and safer. Growing via processes of internal and external expansion, they soon became multi-units, but did not immediately become multinationals. Company success on the domestic market generally came before the process of internationalization, which normally began with exports.

The Second Industrial Revolution, however, created new conditions that drove big business to invest directly abroad in the favorable framework provided by the First Globalization, thus originating multinationals. The sectors affected by the new technological paradigm, whether chemical-related or based on assembly lines, were characterized by high fixed costs and continuous production processes that needed to run smoothly, free of obstacles or interruptions, to avoid diseconomies of scale and damage to their final output. In order to minimize the risk of interruptions and bottlenecks, companies adopted strategies of backward and forward vertical integration.

Although companies tended to favor the domestic market for input procurement, in some cases they could secure direct control of raw or intermediate materials only by investing abroad, and consequently adopted a "resource-seeking" strategy. This is certainly the case of agribusiness (plantations), mining, natural rubber, palm oil and several other natural products. There were several reasons for the choice to internalize the market for raw materials that had existed for centuries. There was the need to avoid the risk of a sudden scarcity of inputs and to take direct control of their supply. This required either a certain degree of technological knowledge to ensure a minimum level of quality, or else meant increasing capital intensity to obtain certain inputs (like oil drilling), to minimize or tackle the risk of increases in trade tariffs, or to react to similar strategies of competitors.

On the other hand, companies also needed to integrate forward and to establish production and sale subsidiaries abroad for "market-seeking" purposes. As mass production spread and the volume of trade started to increase exponentially, FDI became an attractive alternative to exports for both reactive and proactive reasons. Reactive responses were triggered by an external shock that modified the existing scenario and made exports a less attractive option, such as a rise in customs tariffs and other import barriers (from the 1870s), or were triggered by aggressive competition in markets that were by their nature oligopolistic. Proactive reasons, however, are the main explanation for an FDI strategy when the decision to produce abroad was a strategic move in itself, such as when transport costs were excessive (for instance, due to a product's weight, value or perishability), or the local government required the company to set up local facilities, or some adaptation to local conditions was needed, or local agents were unable (or not sufficiently committed) to sell products that were, in some cases, highly sophisticated and technologically advanced (Colli, 2016).

Selection of a suitable location was based on several considerations. For resource-seeking investments, the choice was basically dictated by the geographical location of the resources. However, it was a different situation for manufacturing processes. According to Mira Wilkins, multinationals chose one or another location for reasons such as the number of opportunities provided by a certain market (for example, market potential or the absence of local competitors), political conditions (such as stability, openness towards foreign capital, and the general business climate), geographical and, above all, cultural proximity (including language, emigrant communities and so on), and other indirect considerations like the strategic position of a given nation (Wilkins, 1974).

Unlike their predecessors, companies could now send information and goods relatively quickly and cheaply due to the 19th-century revolution in transportation and communications. This enabled them to apply new coordination techniques to their branches abroad, which were, as a consequence, increasingly closely controlled by the mother company, flexible in their adaptation to local markets, and fully dependent on the home country for both technology and organization. However, multinational companies from different nations enjoyed different competitive advantages. US multinationals generally had a dispersed ownership and were strictly controlled by managerial hierarchies. After a process of domestic expansion they moved abroad, pursuing strategies of backward and forward integration based on competitive advantages related to technology, or else motivated by resource-seeking strategies. On the other hand, although there were significant variations, European companies were generally less eager to adopt bureaucratic structures. On the eve of the First World War, British firms' internationalization was still largely based on free-standing and trading companies; these were usually smaller than their US counterparts, and their founders or their families were still capable of managing them. The internationalization process of German firms was more similar to that of the US firms, although family control often remained more important than managerial hierarchies.

Taking all these factors into account, it is not surprising that Western Europe and the US accounted for over 99 percent of the total of the stock of outward investments during the First Globalization. Developing economies in Latin America, Africa, Asia and the Middle East with abundant natural resources accounted for two-thirds of the total stock of inward investments and were especially attractive to resource-seeking investments. On the other hand, most investments in advanced economies, and also a significant share of investment in countries engaged in intense catching up, concerned manufacturing and services and were essentially market-seeking.

5.5 International business challenged: the first de-globalization in the interwar years and the gradual restoration after the Second World War

The disruption of globalization caused by the First World War had a strong impact on international business. The conflict destroyed the pre-existing equilibrium in global business and forced internationally active companies to face new problems and challenges. Although the conflict actually stimulated internationalization, due to the expansion of production capacity, the increasing importance of technology in generating international competitive advantages, and the incentives for companies to invest abroad to secure necessary inputs, the negative impacts of the war soon became evident.

Attempts to restore at least some features of the pre-war global market in terms of international trade, finance and monetary policies were destined to fail. The severe economic recession immediately after the war, and above all the Great Depression that followed the 1929 economic crisis, in a context of economic, cultural, social and political reaction against globalization, completely changed the framework in which multinationals operated. Rising nationalism spread across the former belligerent nations and then became worldwide. In both industrialized and developing countries, openings turned into barriers, free trade into protection, and "foreignness" into a liability.

Doing business abroad now became very difficult, since nationalist tendencies affected both the establishment and the daily operations of foreign companies. Russia's Soviet revolution and subsequent nationalizations without compensation had shocked the international business community, transforming what had once been a very attractive area for foreign investors into an extremely risky environment. In addition, several other countries were suffering different degrees of political instability, thus increasing the risks for foreign investors. In this framework, dictatorships and authoritarian governments guaranteed a stability that was much appreciated by foreign investors; for instance, direct US investments in manufacturing declined by 48 percent in France during the 1930s, but doubled in Germany during the same decade.

Divestment was a frequent exit decision of both multinationals and free-standing companies. As specific organizational arrangements, these were also rapidly declining in number due to other factors: capital and technologies in developing countries became less necessary; investment in local services was often given to municipality-controlled companies at the end of the concession period; many free-standing companies were active in sectors seriously affected by the decline in international market prices; and new controls on exchange impeded remittance of profits, and so threatened the very aim of the investment itself.

Despite the challenging economic and geopolitical framework of this de-globalization wave, it is worth noticing that multinationals, especially US multinationals, continued to spread. This was due, above all, to the strengthening and dissemination of their unchallenged technological advantages. Foreign subsidiaries of these firms also grew as a result of their tendency to internalize transactions in a context of great market uncertainty and risk; in some cases, the repatriation of profits became so difficult that subsidiaries began to invest locally.

During the interwar years, multinationals were usually organizational entities that transferred assets abroad to obtain economic rents, while foreign subsidiaries were basically "truncated replicas" of the parent company. However, the companies operating abroad needed to develop new strategies and systems to survive in the new framework of de-globalization, so radically different from the previous international context, and to adapt to this hostile environment. Their strategies included cloaking and camouflaging techniques to disguise themselves in markets where foreigners were perceived as threatening national interests; the creation of subsidiaries in neutral countries, such as Switzerland, the Netherlands or Sweden, transforming them into holdings for the mother firm's foreign investments; the adoption of stronger strategic and organizational flexibility and increased efforts to adapt to local political conditions; and the creation of cooperative agreements in the form of international cartels that allowed the persistence of some form of international trade and investment in a de-globalized world. These and other similar strategies of adaptation to the challenging context of the interwar years allowed international business activity to survive and even to expand.

In the decades that followed the Second World War, globalization was gradually – and only partially – reconstructed, given the framework imposed by the Cold War and the process of decolonization. Multinational firms played a key role in the restoration of the global economy during these decades, and in fostering economic growth during the period generally known as the "Golden Age"; they transferred both tangible assets (goods, skilled labor and capital) and intangible assets (technologies, management skills and intellectual property rights) to host countries. However, international companies were impacted again by these new conditions, making adaption to the changes a necessity.

At the end of the war, US dominance was unchallenged in many domains, also due to the downgrading of its major competitors, Europe and Japan, and the isolation of the centrally planned economies. In the US, factors like the presence of antitrust policies that hindered the formation of international cartels, the post-war development of idiosyncratic technological knowledge in some industries (like electronics and pharmaceuticals) and the rapid progress made in communications favored the gradual consolidation of a monolithic organizational model. By the early 1960s, multinational companies were mostly US-based and were characterized by resilient competitive advantages related to new technology. These were extremely large companies that tended to internalize transactions, adopting a strategy of international vertical and/or horizontal integration, and they typically established subsidiaries abroad in order to exploit their technological advantage. The new technological developments reduced monitoring costs, and this enabled company headquarters to exert close control over its foreign subsidiaries, which were consequently obliged to closely follow directives from top management in the home country.

Within a few decades, the successful rebirth of international entrepreneurship in Europe and Japan began to challenge, and then almost to outpace, the US in terms of the stock of FDIs. However, US multinationals and the emerging or re-emerging European and Japanese multinationals were quite heterogeneous; they reflected the specificities of their home and host environments, the features of the industries in which they operated, and their own histories and skills. US multinationals tended to fully own and control their subsidiaries, adopting extremely centralized strategies and structures with a high level of global integration and a low level of local responsiveness; this was the "Global" type of multinational (Bartlett and Ghoshal, 1989). On the other hand, their European counterparts acted more as coordinated federations, in which the parent company granted considerable autonomy to foreign affiliates while exercising control over general strategy and transferring knowledge.

As the markets continued to recover and expand, and international competition increased in an evolving economic context, multinationals began to display an increasing variety of aims, strategies and structures. Adaptation to local markets started to become a remarkable source of advantage, increasing the heterogeneity of approaches to international markets, while at the same time efficiency-seeking and strategic asset-seeking behaviors were partly replacing market-seeking and resource-seeking aims. Multinationals began to look for scale and scope economies in their operations and to use intra-group trading to increase their economic efficiency; this brought corporate integration of activities, leading to big export platforms, foreign investments focused on the production of specific parts or components, or combined procurement of materials. A clear division of labor was occurring between different stages of the value chain, which also considered the difference in international costs, and this gave origin to mergers and acquisitions, divestments in some markets, especially from the 1970s, and cross-border alliances, especially from the 1980s onward.

5.6 Between a new globalization and another de-globalization: multinationals to transnationals (and back?)

With growing intensity from the early 1990s, the present globalization wave put an even stronger emphasis on the borderless diffusion of direct investments. In this newly favorable technological, institutional and cultural framework, multinationals once again had to modify their behavior to deal with the opportunities and the challenges ahead. As in the past, the dynamics of globalization impacted on the business world (and vice versa), shaping the behavior of local and international companies.

By the end of the 20th century, the world's largest firms generated a considerable quota of their output outside their home economies, and their shares were listed on several stock exchanges simultaneously. Despite this, however, the strategies of the largest multinationals continued to be "regional" rather than global. These companies were mostly located within the so-called "Triad" formed by East Asia, Europe and North America. Innovative behaviors coexisted with very traditional strategies and structures. At the turn of the century, mainly due to a further acceleration in the integration process supported by a new information and communications revolution, the strategies and structures of multinational companies began to undergo a radical transformation.

Inflows of FDI toward all developing areas began to increase, while FDI outflows from developing countries boomed from the 2000s onward, alongside a growing number of large corporations in countries like Brazil, Russia, India and China (BRIC). Table 5.1 and Figure 5.1 illustrate these trends.

These dynamics in the volume of foreign investments advanced at the same time as new strategies and organizational forms; keywords included organizational decentralization, specialization and vertical disintegration, modularity, flexibility, knowledge exchange and diffusion, inter-organizational collaboration and openness, and networks. What had been almost exclusively domestic production processes began to be fragmented across borders. The consequent geographical dispersion of the value chain allowed new players to participate in the production process, revolutionizing the relative importance of location factors; this offered remarkable opportunities for emerging economies to catch up and participate in global value chains dispersed around the world.

Table 5.1 BRIC companies in the Fortune Global 500 list

	2007		2022	
	Number	Revenues ($billion)	Number	Revenues ($billion)
Brazil	5	168.6	7	344.778
China	24	838.5	135	11.012.708
India	6	147.5	9	541.571
Russia	4	176	3	313.144

Source: Authors' own elaboration based on Fortune Global 500 (2008 and 2023 editions).

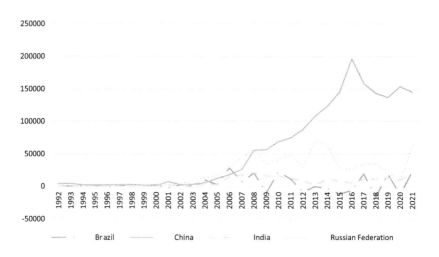

Figure 5.1 FDI outflows from the BRIC countries (US dollars at current prices in millions), 1992–2021

Source: own elaboration based on https://unctadstat.unctad.org/.

The new strategies and new organizational forms adopted by multinational enterprises during the "second globalization" were largely the outcome of several drivers. These include developments in the international institutional environment concerning trade and investment, now emphasizing liberalization, free trade policies, frictionless capital markets and deregulation, and constant improvements in transportation and communication technologies.

First of all, concerning the institutional environment, it must be noted that there was a progressive worldwide trend toward reduction of both tariff and non-tariff barriers after the Second World War. Starting from the 1960s, within the General Agreement on Tariffs and Trade framework, successive rounds of negotiations culminated in the establishment of the World Trade Organization (WTO) in 1995. At the same time, supra-national free trade areas were created, like the European Union (EU, established in 1993 with its origins in the European Economic Community founded in 1957), the North American Free Trade Agreement (now the US–Mexico–Canada Agreement, established in 1994) and Mercosul (or Mercosur, established in 1995). In addition, over time, and especially from the beginning of the new millennium, there was a significant increase in the efficiency of institutions aiming to safeguard international property rights.

Moreover, some countries which had been reluctant to receive foreign investments gradually changed their attitude from the 1960s onward. In Asia, one of the first to move in this sense was the small state of Singapore, which experienced an extraordinary growth spurt in the following decades, mainly due to the new policies adopted by its government. Its development strategy was quite exceptional at the time, characterized by great openness and enormous investments in infrastructure and education so as to develop the ability of local enterprises to absorb foreign knowledge and know-how. Another Southeast Asian country, South Korea, launched a real economic miracle from the 1960s onward by adopting a new outward-looking strategy. A key ingredient of its rapid economic growth was the decision to promote an export-oriented model of industrialization. On the other hand, strong restrictions remained in place on imports of goods from abroad and on FDI.

From the late 1970s and early 1980s onward, privatization and deregulation policies were adopted by several governments across the world, affecting natural monopolies that had once been under the direct supervision of the state, like railroads, airlines and telecommunications, and thus providing interesting opportunities for foreign investors. A true revolution, however, took place in China in the late 1970s, with the beginning of a new "open door" era of reforms, and culminating in the country's membership of the WTO in 2001. The same occurred in Eastern Europe in the 1990s, following the fall of the Berlin Wall, as governments of countries that had belonged to the Communist bloc now adopted policies of export-led growth within the framework of capitalist, liberalized and privatized market economies. Last but not least, India liberalized its policies concerning inward foreign investment and trade in the early 1990s. These openings offered further opportunities for multinational companies, even in business environments with high levels of risk and uncertainty due to factors like corruption, weak protection of property rights, and other institutional voids.

A second element with a considerable impact on international business in this phase was an intense process of innovation in transportation, and above all in communications, which influenced companies' organizational capabilities and impacted on the development of capital-intensive industries through a substantial reduction of risk and uncertainty costs. The speed of information transfer was increased by technological improvements like fiber-optic cables and the spread of personal computers from the 1980s onward. These innovations revolutionized communications, making it possible to relocate parts of the production process (and relative knowledge) to subsidiaries in countries where wages were low. The "Internet Revolution" made it easier for multinationals to organize themselves more efficiently by reducing one of the fundamental incentives to vertical integration: transaction (especially control) costs. From the early 1990s onward, companies massively adopted offshoring strategies, relocating to low-cost countries their most labor-intensive corporate activities, like the production of components and parts, customer services, accounting and human resources, as well as software development and maintenance.

Lastly, within the framework of the "liberal consensus", now free of Cold War tensions, multinationals could once again benefit from a number of cultural and other advantages deriving from their original geographic locations. Cultural similarities operated in the direction of reducing the level of perceived business risk and the transaction costs associated with foreign operations. While the destination of the outward FDI of developed and emerging countries became global during the Second Globalization Wave, it has actually been shown that most companies still preferred to invest in countries with a cultural or geographical proximity to their home economy, at least in the first stage of their international expansion. This was the case of US outward FDI in Canada and Latin America, Japanese FDI in Asia, British FDI in the US, and Portuguese FDI in Brazil. Spanish multinationals looked to Spanish-speaking Latin America when under pressure due to their nation's recent entry into the European Economic Community and the consequent implications in terms of increasing competition and commitment to pursue liberalization policies. For large Spanish companies, investment in Latin American countries offered a context of great cultural and linguistic proximity with attractive growth opportunities before facing the more aggressive competition of the other European states at home. Spanish investments in Latin America were key to enabling the emergence of new global giants, especially in the utilities and banking industries. However, acceptance in the host economies was not always enthusiastic, and anti-Spanish accusations of neo-colonialism were not uncommon. Despite the opportunity offered by a familiar context, investment in former colonies actually proved a difficult experience for many multinationals.

The institutional, technological and cultural drivers that permeated the Second Globalization Wave, together with the multinationals' strategies of global efficiency, national responsiveness and worldwide learning, culminated in the diffusion of a new kind of multinational company, the "transnational" company, which had a high degree of global integration, local responsiveness and knowledge transfer (Bartlett and Ghoshal, 1989). According to the most common definition, a transnational company (TNC) is an enterprise coordinating and operating through a network of largely independent subsidiaries, all with different capabilities, which collaborate by exchanging knowledge and innovations. This model had emerged in previous decades and now boomed during the new globalization phase, making it possible for companies to build their business strategies and organizational structures by leveraging on networks of companies located in geographically dispersed value chains, which over time increased their degree of complexity. During the 1980s, multinationals had operated through networks of subsidiaries that were closely dependent on their parent companies, but the second millennium witnessed the diffusion of "open multinational networks", resulting in increased efficiency and giving an overall competitive advantage. Foreign-owned units played a fundamental role as sources of new ideas and competences. Often local, the decentralized units were entrusted by the parent company with the responsibility for strategic innovation. Multinational companies became more open network structures of geographically distributed centers of value creation. They invested according to the different conditions of specific locations in the host countries and the sources of external knowledge extending beyond the local context. Consequently, companies were often involved in a set of different, close and relatively stable relations with different partners (suppliers and customers); these were not all located in the same place, and each in turn also had other business relationships, so that it was as if companies were sailing in a sea of networks. The increasing liberty of initiative and responsibilities of the sub-units of a transnational organizational form amplified this effect: multinational sub-units themselves created new external business networks and played a central role in linking knowledge from their parent firm or from other sister units with more distant knowledge from their own, local or global, external networks.

One of the best example of this is probably Unilever. Resulting from the merger of a Dutch margarine producer and a British soap-maker in the 1920s, it had favored a loose organizational structure from the very outset. The business areas of this multinational (food, personal care and home care) also fostered this trend in the following decades, since the nature of the company's products allowed it to benefit from economies of scale and appropriate choice of production locations, but at the same time it also required proximity to local markets. The example of tea is telling: this seemingly simple product is drunk hot and diluted with milk in Britain, hot and sugary in the Middle East, and iced in the Americas. Over time, Unilever has built up a sophisticated decentralized organizational structure with the aim of combining local initiative with some centralized control. Today, the structure of the company is organized around five "business groups" (beauty and wellbeing, personal care, home care, nutrition, ice cream), each of which is fully responsible and accountable for its own strategy, growth and profit delivery globally. The company is now at the center of a global network of affiliates and partner suppliers. In 2023, it operated in over 190 countries, had over 300 factories across 69 countries, carried out research and development in six global labs and ten regional hubs, and relied on an ecosystem of 54,000 partner suppliers. According to the company's policies, its partners are encouraged to collaborate with Unilever in generating shared value and in fostering innovation.

Local and global knowledge sourcing were thus complementary in the innovation strategies of multinational firms. The headquarters of the company acted essentially like the conductor of an orchestra, coordinating independent "professionals"; according to some scholars, the dominant view of a company's headquarters as a single unit with a defined geographic identity was becoming obsolete.

To summarize, as in the past and also in this case, new technological revolutions (the Third and, more recently, the Fourth Industrial Revolution), a phase of global economic integration, the liberalization of markets, and deregulation stimulated the energies of both international entrepreneurs and firms, and also expanded the range of organizational types. The main impact of the new environment on global firms was, therefore, the fragmentation of previously hierarchical and integrated structures. They moved toward transnational networks and global value chains that showed an increasing dispersion of organizational authority relations and took advantage of the global division of labor and cost differentials across countries. This more flexible form of organization even challenged the national identity of companies, now transformed into complex networks of geographically dispersed, but interrelated, assets and capabilities.

Not surprisingly, business forms like these, relying so strongly on globalization and its opportunities in terms of free trade and low political barriers to international business, were seriously affected in the late 2000s when globalization began to face challenges again, mostly due to the global financial crisis of 2007–2008 and growing geopolitical tensions in several parts of the world. The US–China trade war, the escalation of tensions between Russia and Ukraine leading to the outbreak of war in 2022, the rise of populism and increasing nationalism in the US and in Europe, the UK's withdrawal from the EU, the geopolitical ambitions of the leaders of Saudi Arabia and the United Arab Emirates, Latin American political divisions, Afghanistan's never-ending conflict, tensions in Syria and the COVID-19 pandemic all were important shocks that impacted indirectly and directly on international business.

Formal and informal trade barriers grew steadily during the 2010s, while companies and products were not treated equally regardless of their origin. The Chinese telecommunications company Huawei, banned or sanctioned in the US and other countries with the claim that it posed a security risk and could facilitate Chinese spying, is probably an extreme example of this trend. Moreover, increasing tensions in the international geopolitical framework meant increased levels of risk for internationally active companies, a situation for which most were ill-prepared. Global value chains began to suffer structural disruption, adding further uncertainty to what were already difficult conditions in the domestic and international markets. This growing complexity, together with a rapid deterioration in the quality of international relations among great powers, has given rise to processes of "reshoring" of investments that were previously located abroad, reducing the "thickness" of value chains, and consequently also the level of interdependencies in the global economy.

Of course, globalization and its creatures, TNCs and global production networks, will not fade away overnight. Nevertheless, the new scenario is of a globalization under serious threat. The drivers and the impacts of this are largely explained in the final chapter of this book, and are exemplified by the US–China trade and technological war and by other dynamics and events such as the Ukraine War. It is now evident that multinationals are holding back on investments, carefully evaluating the international situation, and re-evaluating their behavior with regard to production locations, supply chain organization and the allocation of investment across regions.

Chapter 3 of this book mentioned that A.T. Kearney pioneered globalization indexes in the early 2000s. Interestingly enough, since 2012 this management consulting firm has published an annual Reshoring Index[1] that tracks the main trends in the return of manufacturing companies to the US from 14 low-cost Asian countries and other geographical areas to which sourcing, production and assembly were offshored during recent decades. In its 2022 edition, the report accompanying the index argued that a decade of tracking reshoring and nearshoring activities allows the claim that the combination of the COVID-19 pandemic, trade wars and tariffs, and the ongoing supply chain disruptions have turned what had been a strategic theory into a market reality. According to this study, there had been a steady increase in the number of firms that were moving or had moved their investments back to the US or neighboring countries, Mexico in particular. In addition, companies were now looking at each other to see if it were possible to achieve a critical mass in the reshoring movement so as to build up a local supplier ecosystem, local or in nearby countries, to rival that of China. Naturally, this trend affects not only American companies, but is a global situation. In 2015, the European Commission launched a project aiming to identify, analyze and summarize evidence on the reshoring of manufacturing and other value-chain activities to the EU, showing the growing trend among European companies of relocating their activities to less distant countries, often to countries within the EU itself. According to a study by the consulting firm BCI Global (*Global Reshoring & Footprint Strategy*) and based on a survey submitted to senior level executives of 125 global

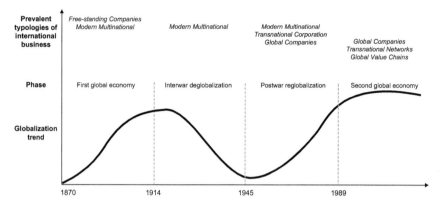

Figure 5.2 Multinational enterprises between two globalizations

companies, over 60 percent of European and US manufacturing companies were expecting to re-shore part of their Asia production by 2025.

In this turbulent phase, multinational companies are, therefore, struggling to find appropriate strategies and structures to deal with a remarkably high level of geopolitical risk in a phase of de-globalization, searching for survival and new growth paradigms. The forefront of international business strategies in the early 2020s is probably relocation in its nuances of onshoring, nearshoring or friendshoring, together with restructuring (which usually means shortening) of the global value chains that international companies once relied on.

This chapter has illustrated how, in the very long term, entrepreneurs and companies have adapted their strategies and organizational structures to changes in the global institutional and political framework, including geopolitical scenarios and attitudes toward foreign multinationals in the host economies, as well as to production and information and communication technology. Figure 5.2 summarizes how different types of multinational organizations emerged in different waves of globalization, from the free-standing companies and modern multinationals that were protagonists of the First Globalization Wave to the global companies and transnational networks which characterized the more recent Second Globalization Wave.

While these models of multinationals have frequently coexisted and overlapped in the past, and still exist today, entrepreneurs and international companies are currently building the strategic and organizational model that will help them navigate the current de-globalization phase.

Note

1 https://www.kearney.com/service/operations-performance-transformation/us-reshoring-index.

References

Rolv Petter Amdam and Ove Bjarnar, "Globalization and the development of two industrial clusters: Comparing two Norwegian clusters, 1900–2010", *Business History Review*, 89(4), 2015: 693–716.

Christopher A. Bartlett and Sumantra Ghoshal, *Managing Across Borders: The Transnational Solution*. Boston: Harvard Business School Press, 1989.

Buck Consultants International (BCI) and Supply Chain Media, *Global Reshoring & Footprint Strategy*, March 24, 2022.

Catherine Casson, "Guilds", in Teresa da Silva Lopes, Christina Lubinski, Heidi J.S. Tworek (eds.), *The Routledge Companion to the Makers of Global Business*, London: Routledge, 2019: 159–170.

Andrea Colli, *Dynamics of International Business: Comparative Perspectives of Firms, Markets and Entrepreneurship*. New York: Routledge, 2016.

Teresa da Silva Lopes, Christina Lubinski, and Heidi J. S. Tworek (eds.), *The Routledge Companion to the Makers of Global Business*. New York: Routledge, 2019.

Robert Fitzgerald, *The Rise of the Global Company: Multinationals and the Making of the Modern World (New Approaches to Economic and Social History)*. Cambridge: Cambridge University Press, 2016.

Fortune, *Fortune Global 500* (special issue), 21 July 2008.

Fortune, *Fortune Global 500* (special issue), 2 August 2023.

Geoffrey Jones, *Multinationals and Global Capitalism: From the Nineteenth to the Twenty-First Century*. New York: Oxford University Press, 2005.

Mira Wilkins, *The Maturing of Multinational Enterprise: American Business Abroad from 1914 to 1970*. Cambridge: Harvard University Press, 1974.

Chapter 6

Global Leviathans

6.1 Governments and globalization

As the previous chapter has shown, globalization has had, and continues to have, a powerful impact on the structures, strategies and performances of both domestic and international firms. It has also shown how multinational companies have historically been among the drivers that promoted globalization itself. The aim of this chapter is to include another important player of a different nature – national governments, which are, and have constantly been in the past, powerful agents in the ongoing process of global integration.

Governments can play a pivotal role on at least two levels. The first level has already been analyzed in depth in Chapter 4, and is the role that governments play in providing the institutional and regulatory framework: the complex of rules, laws and policies that facilitate (or prevent) one polity's access to globalization. Governments' regulation of trade, of foreign direct investments, their control over capital flows, liberalization and privatization, and also their regulation of migration flows directly affect how their countries take part in the globalization process. Moreover, government actions and policies are powerful elements directly influencing the "location advantages" of a host country, and therefore the locational choices of multinational companies. For example, the government is responsible for the creation and functioning of an efficient legal framework protecting foreign investments and property rights, for the country's infrastructural endowment that makes it attractive to foreign investors, and for the educational system that makes good-quality human resources available. Finally, another major contribution of the government to a country's access to the global community is the strength and quality of its international relations, which ultimately affect the level of geopolitical risk, with a direct impact on the overall stability of the global scenario.

DOI: 10.4324/9780429490255-6

Secondly, governments can become important players on the global scenario by directly investing in the ownership of companies. On the one hand, they can channel national wealth into the direct ownership of foreign companies abroad. This is the case of sovereign wealth funds (SWFs), which are state-owned investment funds endowed with financial resources generated by the government's activities; these are currently proliferating as prominent international investors. SFWs are growing steadily in terms of numbers, deals and value of assets. According to the 2021 *Sovereign Wealth Funds Report*, SWFs currently manage more than 10 trillion dollars in assets. This means that if they were, on an aggregate base, an actual country, they would rank third behind China and the US. In some cases, national governments direct SWFs to acquire very significant stakes in private firms and thus to exert a relevant impact on their behavior and strategic choices. Norway's Government Pension Fund Global and the China Investment Corporation, two of the world's largest SWFs, are good examples in this sense.

The aim of this chapter, however, is to focus on a different kind of state ownership, which is usually more strictly linked to an effective and persistent control of the company: the state ownership of domestic firms that are keenly involved in international activities.

6.2 State-owned enterprises in international markets

Both in the recent past and increasingly in the present, states have been directly involved in various ways in the ownership of companies that are not only some of the world's largest multinationals, but also exert – like the private companies – a significant influence on the process of integration itself (see for instance Cuervo-Cazzurra ed., 2017). The following pages will focus on the dynamics, reasons and main implications of the internationalization of these large state-owned corporations, often referred to in business literature as "Leviathans", a term borrowed from Thomas Hobbes' renowned treatise.

Far from disappearing after the intense and widespread wave of privatizations between the mid-1980s and the end of the century, state-owned enterprises remain a permanent feature of today's capitalist economies around the world. Their diffusion is, of course, still heavily influenced by the degree of development of the domestic economy in which they operate, although even developed countries have recently displayed willingness to resort to forms of direct state control over companies operating in strategic industries. Between 2008 and 2018, the share of state-owned assets among the world's 2,000 largest firms doubled to 20 percent (Vitor et al., 2020), and in 2022 their assets represented roughly 50 percent of global gross domestic product (GDP) (Manuilova et al., 2022).

The most recent turbulence in the global economic framework, from the 2007–2008 financial crisis up to the COVID-19 pandemic, has caused a recession wave that has renewed the legitimization of direct government intervention through various instruments, including state-controlled enterprises. A recent World Bank note describes, for instance, how state-owned enterprises can play a crucial countercyclical role if they are able to effectively deal with the main issues that have historically characterized this form of company.

Additionally, an important number of the largest state-controlled companies are today multinationals. In 2019, 16 of the 100 largest globally active multinationals were under government control, in several cases displaying forms of mixed ownership where the state's direct ownership was counterbalanced by the presence of retail and institutional investors. An important issue in this respect – with a significant impact on the relationship between state-owned multinationals and the global economy – is that the present form of state ownership, its rationales, strategies and the governance structures it originates, are in several cases quite different from those of the past.

6.3 The rise and fall of state-owned enterprises between de-globalization and re-globalization

Although there are cases of companies directly owned by governments that were founded in past centuries as state monopolies in mining or in strategic sectors like shipbuilding, their economic significance peaked during the 20th century (Millward, 2005; Toninelli, 2000). Of course, state-owned companies played – and sometimes still play – a crucial role in socialist countries like modern China. With regard to the capitalistic world in particular, state-owned enterprises in their "modern" form appeared in the West along with the de-globalization wave and the phase of economic depression and interventionist policies that marked the interwar years. State-owned enterprises and holdings emerged either from the nationalization of previously private assets or from the establishment of completely new firms. In general, national governments considered the direct ownership of productive assets as an efficient multi-purpose tool. It was useful for promoting investments in strategic industries, especially energy, infrastructures and armaments, to cope with natural monopolies, to relocate production capacity and promote employment in depressed areas, and to pursue other goals concerning national welfare and economic progress, often in a purely "mercantilist" perspective. Of course, the strategies and managerial philosophies of these companies were influenced by the political climate of the period, characterized by a pervasive nationalism fueled by populist governments oriented toward protection of the national economy and autarkic policies.

Notwithstanding what were often the good intentions of wise policymakers, economic efficiency soon became only one of the aims, and not generally the principal aim, of the state-owned enterprises, which frequently had to incorporate various ideological, political or military constraints into their decisional framework.

The years of post-war recovery and of subsequent rapid economic growth witnessed a further expansion of state-owned enterprises. Most companies in the developed capitalist economies significantly expanded their range of action into activities no longer related to their original spheres of operation, in an endless struggle between achieving political mandates and economic efficiency. During the 1950s and 1960s in particular, state-owned companies were rightfully considered one of the major pillars of postwar economic miracles. In Europe, they built and managed key infrastructures in transport and communications, contributed greatly to their respective countries' total fixed investments (on average, 30–40 percent of the total in the major European economies from the second half of the 1950s to the mid-1960s), and also played a central role in promoting research and technological advancement. According to some estimates, European governments funded almost 50 percent of the research and development budgets of their respective countries through the laboratories of state-owned enterprises (Anastassopoulos et al., 1987). Outside the socialist countries' centrally planned economies, state-owned enterprises provided a fundamental contribution to the processes of economic convergence and technological catching up in the so-called Third World countries from the 1960s onward. In most former colonies of the West in Africa and South-East Asia, state-owned enterprises, often the result of nationalization of colonizers' assets, became powerful drivers of the economic growth and development of their respective countries, in some cases providing the necessary stimulus to private entrepreneurship. Large and very large state-owned enterprises, in any case, remained mostly a Western European phenomenon. In 1962, according to data from Dunning and Pearce, 13 of the world's 400 largest enterprises were state-owned companies, 12 of which also had their headquarters in Western Europe; by 1972, the number had risen to 23, with 16 based in Western Europe; and in 1982 the number was 52, of which 37 were Western European (Dunning and Pearce, 1985).

In this historical phase, state-owned companies frequently adopted an approach that could considerably limit and hinder globalization. In many cases, they took direct responsibility for developing advanced technologies that were still absent in their own country, with the clear intent of preventing the entrance of foreign multinationals in that field. Sometimes multinational companies in an advanced industry were accepted only if they agreed to establish a joint venture with a local state-owned company. This behavior limited the foreign firms' freedom of operation and was quite common, especially in emerging markets like those of Latin America. In other cases, state-owned companies intervened to rescue a domestic firm from possible takeover by a foreign multinational. In the late 1960s and 1970s, for example, the Italian state-owned holding IRI took over several private companies in the food industry for this very purpose. Although in an indirect way, state-owned companies thus often played an active role against a strengthening of globalization trends, at least in terms of allowing foreign competitors into their country.

Despite a prevalently domestic orientation, a few of the state-owned companies had also progressively begun to engage in value-adding activities outside their home countries; this was typical of the energy sector, in which European state-owned enterprises progressively internationalized their activities. Between 1965 and 1985, the rising number of state-owned multinationals proceeded alongside an increasing heterogeneity of their activities, as Table 6.1 shows.

By the mid-1980s the multinational outreach of state-owned enterprises was no longer limited to a few exceptional cases, but the phenomenon was still relatively limited. Most of the multinational state-owned companies outside the US remained focused on the energy sector, especially oil, and on metals and mechanical engineering activities. Most, moreover, had a Western European nation as their country of origin, with France, Germany and Italy as the main countries involved.

Overall, and particularly in the Western world, the public opinion of state-owned companies progressively became openly critical, particularly after the negative economic cycle of the 1970s – since capital, labor and energy-intensive processes were typically performed by state-owned enterprises and these were mostly affected by the rise in input costs. Their chronic inefficiency and the persistence of political clientelism made it increasingly necessary to carry out a process of restructuring, followed by ambitious privatization processes as launched by British Conservative governments from the early 1980s onward. The radical change in the way state-owned enterprises were perceived is partially explained by the concomitant impact of two exogenous factors.

Firstly, a new wave of technological innovations weakened the foundations of what had once been natural monopolies traditionally operated by state-owned enterprises. Secondly, technological advancements were further legitimized

Table 6.1 State-owned enterprises among the world's 2,000 largest industrial companies outside the US

Rank	Enterprise	Sectors of activity	Country of origin
		1965	
3	British Petroleum	Oil products	UK
18	Renault	Automobiles	France
33	ENI	Oil products	Italy
		1975	
10	ENI	Oil products, chemicals, textiles	Italy
13	Renault	Automobiles, tractors, machine tools	France
37	British Leyland	Automobiles	UK
65	DSM	Chemicals, fertilizers, plastics	Netherlands
70	Salzgitter	Iron and steel industry, machine tools, shipyards	Germany
94	Voest-Alpine	Iron and steel industry	Austria
108	Statfortag	Steel, mining, paper products, tobacco	Sweden
185	VIAG	Aluminum, chemicals, electricity	Germany
		1985	
3	IRI	Iron and steel industry, aeronautics, shipyards, electronics, telecommunications	Italy
4	ENI	Oil products, chemicals	Italy
10	Elf-Aquitaine	Oil products, chemicals	France
18	Petrobras	Oil products	Brazil
28	Kuwait Petroleum	Oil products	Kuwait
29	Voest-Alpine	Metals, machine tools	Austria
30	Renault	Automobiles	France
48	Compagnie Générale d'Electricité	Electrical, electronic engineering	France
54	Saint-Gobain	Glass, cast iron, building materials	France
57	DSM	Chemicals, fertilizers, plastics	France
61	Thomson	Electrical, electronic engineering	France
72	Rhône-Poulenc	Chemicals	France
101	Norsk-Hydro	Oil products, chemicals	Norway
103	YPF	Oil products	Argentina
126	Péchiney	Aluminum	France
133	Aérospatiale	Aircraft industry	France
168	Salzgitter	Iron and steel industry, shipyards	Germany
171	EFIM	Metals, mechanical engineering	Italy

Source: Authors' own elaboration based on Anastassopoulos et al. (1987), pp. 13–15.

by the widespread success and adoption of neoliberal economic policies, which considered active government intervention as a major disturbance of natural market forces. The joint action of international and supranational institutions and organizations, such as the European Economic Community (EEC), the Organization for Economic Cooperation and Development and the World Bank, which aimed to eradicate barriers to trade, strongly pushed in the direction of dismantling the entire system of public enterprise. The Uruguay Round, the eighth round of multilateral trade negotiations within the General Agreement on Tariffs and Trade framework, which took place in 1986 with the participation of 123 nations, reinforced the principle that barriers to trade had to be removed. Among other things, the liberalization process meant necessary improvements in the efficiency of domestic markets that were increasingly impacted by foreign competition. The recipe of the so-called Washington Consensus was therefore gradually extended from developing countries and Latin America to the rest of the world, including the former Communist bloc. One of the key ingredients of this recipe was privatization of state-owned companies, considered as mostly suboptimal forms of business. In the World Bank's publication *Bureaucrats in Business* (1995), inefficient state-owned companies were even accused of slowing down the eradication of poverty in the world.

Europe provides a good example of one of the major battlefields where the war against state-owned companies was fought out in the last decade of the 20th century. In previous decades, the European Commission had tolerated the persistence of state-owned enterprises inside most EEC member states, but now quickly changed direction. The purpose of the Single European Market Act (1986) was to dismantle barriers to free trade within the EEC by the end of 1992, and it marked an important watershed in this respect. The EEC identified the Single Market as the main tool for international competition. Member states were pressured to eliminate each form of protection from competition inside the Union, particularly in natural monopolies and utilities, and these were progressively opened up to market competition. On top of the general forces driving the progressive dismantling of the state-owned enterprise system, it must not be forgotten that their generally very poor performance made state-owned enterprises a heavy burden on the state budget. Privatizations could thus bring additional resources into the state coffers, allowing governments to shift public spending onto other purposes while at the same time meeting the criteria of the Maastricht Treaty for joining the single currency (Clifton et al., 2013).

6.4 Privatizations and globalization: the new "Leviathans"

This new attitude toward former state-owned national "champions" paved the way for a vast program of privatizations, and during the 1980s and 1990s this took on the semblance of a truly global phenomenon, starting with the radical reforms introduced in the UK by the Conservative government of Margaret Thatcher.

Despite its large scale and scope, the privatization process differed significantly from country to country, due to specific local constraints and political institutions that determined the speed of the process, its spread and the ownership structure of the newly privatized companies. This worldwide trend was much more characteristic of the developed economies than of the emerging countries, and mainly affected network utilities, such as airlines, railways, electricity supply and telecommunications, as well as manufacturing, construction, banking and finance, and to a lesser extent also mining. The privatization process peaked in the mid-1990s, when about 600 former state-owned enterprises were privatized each year worldwide (Musacchio and Lazzarini, 2014).

However, this number dropped to around 200 per year at the start of the new millennium, when the limits of the process were becoming evident. While the privatization trend was generally fading, it became obvious that many of the world's large companies had not been privatized at all, or else that they had gone through a process of only partial privatization. Governments continued to hold company shares directly or indirectly through various investment devices, such as state-owned holding companies, development banks, sovereign wealth funds and many others. In emerging markets in particular, state-owned enterprises were still prevalent at all levels of economic development. In 2011, at the end of roughly two decades of global privatizations, over 10 percent of the world's largest companies were still under some form of state ownership (either full or partial), and state-owned enterprises contributed 10 percent of global GDP (Bruton et al., 2015).

This does not mean that the state-owned companies of the new millennium were the same as the old ones, although in some cases they did not change their names or ownership assets. At least four factors concurred to radically transform many of them, making them structurally different from their ancestors.

Firstly, the criticisms and attacks that state-owned companies experienced during the last decades of the 20th century drove most of them, at least in the Western world, to radically change their *modus operandi*, especially in relation to the pursuit of economic efficiency.

Secondly, the concept of state ownership itself had changed profoundly in several countries and industries. In many cases, governments had progressively abandoned the idea of exerting exclusive control over companies not directly connected to strategic industries or to socially sensitive natural monopolies. This meant the acceptance of minority or majority private shareholders, which inevitably meant the adoption of new strategies that were more suitable for profit-seeking private investors. Transformation of the ownership structures of the new state-owned companies often took place within the framework of renewal of the corporate governance rules of these firms, and this was also favored by the entrance of new private shareholders, who required stronger protection of their interests and a greater degree of transparency.

Thirdly, deregulation and liberalization of sectors in which state-owned companies had operated monopolies or had been dominant players implied that these companies now faced a sharp increase in competition, leading them to seek new strategies and management structures. Politicians gradually turned to the new orthodoxy of neoliberalism, while public bureaucrats began to follow the theories of New Public Management (NPM), which basically claimed that the inefficiencies of state-owned corporations could be solved by applying the market-based management rules of the private sector. Inspired by neoliberal perspectives, NPM held that deregulation would provide a powerful instrument to expose these formerly protected sectors to market competition and dynamics, thus increasing the performance and efficiency of all companies in general.

Lastly, in addition to this, the process of privatization historically overlapped and largely intertwined with the second globalization wave, which peaked at the turn of the millennium. The new global dynamics impacted greatly on the behavior of companies that had undergone or were now undergoing a process of partial or complete privatization, as well as on firms that remained entirely in state ownership, transforming their paradigms and shaping the emergence of strategies and structures that were quite new for these enterprises. In fact, as shown in the previous chapters of this book, the acceleration in the global integration of markets after the end of the Cold War had created a framework uniquely favorable to strategies of internationalization that went hand-in-hand with the restructuring of most of the former state-owned companies' ownership and governance structures and their overall business approach.

The interconnection between partial or complete privatization, liberalization and globalization in the Western world has been especially evident in the case of sectors like utilities, telecommunications and banking. In these sectors, the process of liberalization taking place in their home markets forced several former national monopolists to look for new business opportunities abroad, exploiting competences developed on the domestic market or using foreign markets to grow and become more competitive in the new international framework. One good example of this is the Spanish company Repsol, now one of the largest players in the global oil and gas sector. Spain's oil industry had been strictly regulated from the 1920s onward, and the sector remained an inefficient combination of private and state-owned companies up to the 1970s, with a monopoly in the distribution phase, state concessions and centrally established prices. Spain's entry into the EEC in 1986 meant that it had to accept foreign competition and respect European rules that required privatizations and liberalizations. As a response, the Spanish government decided to create some national champions to compete in this new framework. Oil was considered one of the most strategic industries, and efforts were made to establish a company not only able to survive foreign competition at home, but also to be successful on the global market. As a first step, the Spanish government gathered its activities in this field under the umbrella of a state-owned holding, the Instituto Nacional de Hidrocarburos (INH). After a rationalization of these state-owned oil-related assets, Repsol was created in 1987 with INH as its sole shareholder. To increase the company's efficiency, Repsol was privatized, and it adopted a strategy of related diversification and internationalization, with a multidivisional organizational structure. Repsol's shares went public between 1989 and 1997, quoted on both the Madrid and New York stock exchanges. In the mean time, Royal Decree 4/1991 formally ended the existence of the monopoly. By 1999, Repsol was a completely privately owned company adopting modern strategies and structures. Its process of international expansion, considered indispensable to its survival among the oil giants, and its competitiveness and success in the new framework boomed during the following decade via a series of mergers and acquisitions in Latin and North America, Africa and Russia.

Similar dynamics occurred in the cases of companies that remained completely or partly under government control. The Italian energy company Enel, for instance, had held the monopoly for the generation and distribution of electricity in Italy from its creation in 1962 with the nationalization of the electricity industry. The liberalization process that began in the 1990s completely revolutionized the competitive scenario. In the mean time, Enel had changed its status from that of a public agency to a joint-stock company, and was now driven to pursue a strategy of progressive internationalization with the acquisition of foreign competitors in recently deregulated markets. In 1999, the company started a process of partial privatization and further reinforced its strategy of international expansion, accompanied by a diversification of its energy sources, moving from traditional energy sources to renewables and also nuclear. Similarly, the telecommunications sector shows quite effectively how technology, in particular the new digital wireless applications, could quickly undermine the monopoly of public networks.

In the early stages of this process, not all governments were enthusiastic about the foreign expansion of state-owned multinational enterprises. Three main attitudes could be identified in the early 2010s. One of these made the government a possible obstacle to internationalization because it considered the foreign expansion of a big national player as a potential threat to national interests. This was the case with Italy, where there was recurrent concern about the possible impact on local employment of these large companies' foreign investments. A second attitude considered internationalization an important opportunity. Governments with this attitude became big supporters of internationalization, as with China's "Go Global" policy. The third attitude was that some governments were apparently indifferent to the foreign expansion of their state-owned enterprises. In some cases, however, they did actually provide guidance on the developmental impact of outward foreign direct investments, as with Swedish energy company Vattenfall in Africa. Furthermore, it must also be remembered that in some cases, especially after the financial crisis that began in 2007–2008, governments had to bail out failing multinationals, which consequently became state-owned companies.

Whatever the initial attitude of their respective governments, data demonstrating the diffusion and importance of state-owned companies on the global scene are striking, particularly after decades of privatization policies. According to the United Nations Conference on Trade and Development (UNCTAD) *World Investment Report*, a clear majority of the world's state-owned multinationals in the mid-2010s were still completely (34 percent) or prevalently (29 percent) owned by their national governments, with private investors playing a relatively minor role in ownership of these firms' assets (UNCTAD, 2017). In the late 2010s, not only had state-owned companies not entirely disappeared, but they had actually become some of the main actors in international business, playing a pivotal role in economic and geopolitical terms.

In this new framework, scholars have analyzed with great interest the strategies (in some cases aggressive) of internationalization pursued by both minority and majority (or fully) state-owned multinationals. Recent studies have argued that in several cases state-owned multinationals did not underperform compared to their private counterparts. Aldo Musacchio, Felipe Monteiro and Sergio Lazzarini, for instance, basing their analysis on a cross-industry and cross-country database of publicly traded state-owned and private multinationals, argue that state-owned multinationals did not underperform at all when compared to private firms in their return on assets ratio. This could also have been due to the fact that the state is a long-term, patient investor and does not have the same need for profits as private firms. This is especially true of countries with strong political institutions that avoided exerting a disproportionate amount of government power over company strategy, thus also avoiding consequent clashes of aims and agency issues (Musacchio et al., 2018).

Moreover, in a provocative article based on analysis of the impact of state ownership on different forms of invention across distinct institutional and industrial contexts in emerging and developed countries, Sergio Lazzarini, Luis Mesquita, Felipe Monteiro and Aldo Musacchio showed how state ownership can have a positive impact on inventive output under certain institutional conditions. This is also because money can be invested in areas the market is not interested in, at least in the short term. In any case, good governance is critical, and makes a great difference to the heterogeneous financial and innovation performances of different state-owned multinationals (Lazzarini et al., 2020).

6.5 State-owned multinationals: features and dynamics

State-owned multinationals are at present a global phenomenon, with an extremely wide variety of ownership structures, corporate governance practices, strategies and structures. This is largely due also to the differences in the circumstances under which they originated and currently operate in diverse geographical contexts and industries. These companies vary in size, sector of activity, complexity and sophistication. This section will briefly discuss some of the main features of their ownership structures, organizational forms and internationalization strategies.

First of all, with regard to the ownership structure of state-owned multinationals, it is worth mentioning that while some state-owned companies have a combination of public and private ownership, others are still basically an arm of the government. State ownership of the firms currently pursuing an internationalization strategy can be total, majority or minority holdings. The minimum ownership threshold for a company to be defined as state-owned is, of course, subjective. Governments can exert *de facto* control over a company even with a minority share in the enterprise, and several international comparative databases consider state-owned companies to be those in which the government holds a very small quota of the shares. As shown above, since the last decades of the 20th century, governments have often progressively reduced their direct ownership down to the minimum threshold necessary to keep firm control over company strategies. However, this is especially true for Western state-owned corporations, while Asian or Latin American state-owned multinationals are more likely to be under complete or majority state ownership.

Secondly, with regard to organizational typology, state-owned companies were organized approximately in one of four ways after the end of the Second World War: as sections or agencies in a government department, as legal entities separate from government, but called public establishments or corporations, as joint-stock companies with partial or complete state ownership or as municipal companies. Since the beginning of the privatization process, many state-owned companies have been corporatized, and this is usually the case with the largest state-owned multinationals in the world. Also in this case, however, the legal status of state-owned enterprises still varies greatly among sectors and nations. In many countries, for instance, the state-owned companies owned by subnational governments or by municipalities to provide services like local transport or water supply often outnumber the state-owned companies owned by central government. As will be seen, this kind of state-owned company is usually less likely to adopt a strategy of internationalization.

A third feature concerns state-owned companies' foreign direct investment activity. In the case of state-owned companies, even a relatively limited foreign presence has been considered sufficient to identify companies as state-owned multinationals. Anastassopoulos, Blanc and Dussage, for instance, in a pioneering work on state-owned multinationals published in the late 1980s, held that a 10 percent minimum threshold of the corporate turnover derived from foreign activities and operations abroad in at least three countries was the necessary condition for the designation of a company as a state-owned multinational (Anastassopoulos et al., 1987). However, more than the percentage of total turnover generated abroad or the number of countries in which these firms operate, it is important to understand the general strategic perspective that a company under government control adopts when it decides to pursue certain international activities. For example, the decision to invest abroad to exploit natural resources or to open commercial subsidiaries is different from an internationalization strategy based on the establishment of production facilities or the decentralization of strategic functions at a global level, taking advantage of the creation of a network of strategic material and immaterial assets and managing a global value chain. Overall, during recent decades, the internationalization process of former state-owned national champions has become increasingly intense at a global level in both "quantitative" and "qualitative" terms.

In a recent investigation of the drivers that foster the process of internationalization of state-owned companies, Álvaro Cuervo-Cazurra and Cheng Li analyzed four variables that could explain the different propensities of state-owned firms to undertake international ventures, as well as the intensity and direction of this effort (Cuervo-Cazurra and Li, 2022). First of all, they claimed that the industry in which these companies operate might play a relevant role, suggesting that the state-owned companies created to favor the industrial upgrading of their home country are more likely to expand abroad than those established to provide public goods and services. The state-owned companies in the first category were established, for instance, in Europe after the Second World War or in emerging countries that pursued import-substitution strategies in the following decades, and in fact had various incentives to go abroad to obtain assets like advanced technology or to achieve economies of scale. On the other hand, companies set up to provide public services tend to be domestically focused because they basically aim only to solve internal issues by providing services to local communities. Secondly, according to Cuervo-Cazurra and Li, the type of state ownership plays a role in determining the internationalization path of a state-owned company, making state-owned companies owned by higher-level governments like the central administration much more prone to invest abroad than those owned by lower-level governments like municipalities. Central or federal governments tend to facilitate what are considered "national champions", providing them with greater access to political, economic and geopolitical resources in order to help them achieve their purposes, while lower-level governments can provide much less support to their firms in any process of foreign expansion.

The third driver said to impact on the internationalization of state-owned companies is identified as the level of state ownership. In this case, state-owned companies with lower levels of state ownership are more likely to go abroad than their counterparts with higher levels of state ownership. This could be because a higher level of government control of a company could encourage it to pursue more non-market objectives and limit its level of competitiveness abroad, while a higher level of control by politicians and the implementation of non-business objectives could then channel resources towards internal investments to support the reputation of politicians.

Building on this, finally, the managerial independence of state-owned companies is said to play a pivotal role in fostering internationalization strategy of these firms, in that state-owned companies with higher managerial independence would be more likely to invest abroad than those companies with a lower degree of managerial independence. In a state-owned company, in fact, politicians act as principals who ask managers, as their agents, to achieve various aims. This could create a possible conflict of agency due to divergent interests of the two parties. While some governments exert a low level of control over their companies and establish barriers between politicians and managers to prevent politicians from pushing for the pursuit of non-economic aims, other governments exert high levels of control over managers, both directly (for instance, through mandates) or indirectly. The level of managerial independence can also depend on the stage in the life cycle of a company, with managers becoming more independent as the company grows and matures.

According to Cuervo-Cazurra and Li, state-owned companies over which government exerts a high degree of control might have minor incentives to internationalize their activities; for instance, politicians could prefer domestic investments that are more visible to the local population, or international investments may be detrimental to domestic investments. On the other hand, a higher level of managerial independence means that managers are freer to implement strategies that are more aligned with the aims and success of the company, including taking advantage of global opportunities by pursuing a process of internationalization.

The more traditional state-owned multinationals with a high level of state ownership and control today coexist not only with a new model of state-owned enterprise that emerged as a legacy of the privatization decades and has been described in the previous pages, but also with a large number of intermediate situations. If the traditional model of state ownership that was much more common in the past but has not disappeared today is based on a close relationship with the political sphere, and one of the important assets of top management is its political connections, in the case of the "new" state ownership model the main assets of top management are their professional skills and international standing. Both models of state-owned companies have political economy goals. However, while the goals of traditional state-owned companies are limited to enhancing internal consensus and the company is not considered a tool for managing international relations, the political economy goals of the new state-owned enterprises involve both domestic internal consensus and international political standing, including geopolitical purposes, as the next section will discuss.

6.6 State-owned multinationals and globalization: problems and issues

As the previous section has shown in depth, direct ownership of companies by national governments has not disappeared, despite the massive privatization process of the last few decades. In several cases, state-owned companies are still considered to be effective tools for solving issues related to growth and regional imbalances. Some governments maintain a direct ownership stake to avoid the risk of foreign acquisition, particularly in the case of companies operating in industries of primary national interest. In structural determinants, contingent factors also played a role. The financial crisis of 2007–2008 paved the way for a partial comeback of state-owned corporations. Governments intervened to rescue national leaders, companies that were considered "too big to fail" (for instance, in the banking sector). The COVID-19 pandemic and the threats posed by the economic and geopolitical dynamics of the early 2020s contributed to a further acceleration of this trend. To various extents, many governments are now even openly pursuing policies of partial re-nationalization of privatized companies, for instance in the utility and energy sectors.

Of course, it is in the emerging economies, much more than in Western countries, that state-owned enterprises still play a very prominent role. In 2010, China had the highest share of state-owned enterprises among its largest companies, although China's state-owned companies are usually considered less innovative and efficient than their private equivalents and are often accused of the same failings that Western, especially former state-owned, enterprises faced several decades ago.

In addition, this chapter has emphasized the transformation that the present globalization has operated on the traditional model of the state-owned domestic monopolist, showing how significant changes in the governance, organizational structures and degree of internationalization gave origin to a new economic actor, the "partially state-owned multinational". In 2019, according to the UNCTAD *World Investment Report*, European state-owned multinationals accounted for little over one third of all the world's state-owned enterprises, while another 45 percent were located in China and other developing Asian economies (UNCTAD, 2019).

While the previous paragraphs have outlined the dynamics of change in the nature and structure of state-owned enterprises during the present globalization process, they have not highlighted one potentially important aspect of this transformation. In fact, the internationalization of state-owned companies can be considered both an opportunity and a threat.

Domestic governments usually consider state-owned multinational enterprises an opportunity, since they can still play the role of powerful instruments for "old" purposes that combine social, economic, political and strategic interests. State-owned multinationals are also increasingly seen as potentially important instruments of political economy, sometimes used by their own governments for geopolitical purposes. In a recent study, Clegg, Voss and Tardios argued, for instance, that the magnitude and direction of state-owned multinational enterprises can largely depend on the pursuit of a mercantilist domestic agenda by governments, and that autocratic home countries have the opportunity to "re-purpose" state-owned multinationals to pursue international nationalist objectives much more successfully than democracies because they maintain effective control over their state-owned companies (Clegg et al., 2018).

State ownership, on the other hand, presents advantages and disadvantages both for the company itself and for the external environment in which it operates.

With regard to the state-owned multinational's internal perspective, the presence of the government as an owner can provide privileged access, for instance to natural resources and government concessions, as well as subsidized credit and special tax regimes. The impact of these dynamics is, of course, especially maximized in those countries where these advantages are still legally pursuable. However, the "advantages of stateness" can be indirect. For instance, private creditors might offer more favorable conditions to a state-owned company than to a private counterpart, and they might expect the government to step in to rescue the state-owned company if necessary. On the other hand, the presence of the government in the ownership structure of a company can also be a serious threat for the firm, as several recent studies based on empirical evidence show.

State-owned multinationals, in fact, might suffer from a "liability of stateness" because host country governments or citizens might discriminate against them. Other investigations highlighted that state-owned firms encounter higher expectations and pressures than their counterparts in the private sector due to their very nature and to the benefits they are supposed to provide to their owner. Moreover, the presence of the government in the ownership of a company could also represent a threat because it could influence the geographical direction of company expansion. For instance, some studies show that state-owned multinational companies are more prone to expand in riskier host countries (for example, those that are more corrupt or with a weaker rule of law), in some case putting this criterion before business and economic considerations, since they are sure of having the support of their national government and its diplomatic protection.

This leads us to discuss another issue related to state ownership of multinationals: the risk of an excessively politicized and bureaucratic management. The process of internationalization in itself, in this sense, could be seen as a strategy consciously undertaken by top management to escape government control. In fact, according to Anastassopoulos, Blanc and Dussage, among the main challenges facing top management of a state-owned enterprise in the internationalization of the company's activity, the first concerns the extent or degree of freedom of action it can obtain. The second challenge regards the ability of top management to transform and/or adapt the prevailing organizational culture to the new international environment (Anastassopoulos et al., 1987).

The third challenge regards the issue of external private investors in state-owned multinational firms. Minority shareholders could in fact opt to invest in a state-owned multinational enterprise because there are countervailing privileges derived from partnership with the government, and several countries impose enhanced corporate governance and legal constraints to limit abuses by the majority shareholder. However, minority shareholders might fear that the political and, in general, extra-economic purposes related to state ownership could generate agency issues. The equilibrium among different shareholders and stakeholders is at the same time both a challenge (given the different nature and purpose of their holdings) and fundamental, allowing the firm to be efficient and to achieve its goals. Neither listing on a stock exchange nor the presence of private investors can solve the problem of political meddling in a state-owned multinational company. Nonetheless, carefully designed systems of corporate governance can at least mitigate any political interference that might damage minority investors and the company's performance in general. Another study has also shown that the stronger the activity of monitoring and influencing the activities of a state-owned multinational company by civil society and its minority shareholders, the more unlikely it is that the company's decision-makers will pursue self-serving motives; thus, the company's strategies will be more similar to the behavior of wholly privately owned firms. However, the ability of civil society and of minority shareholders to monitor and influence the corporate decision-makers is strongly determined by national institutions. These include informal (such as cultural traditions, customs and religious norms) and formal (codified rules, for instance on property rights) norms and governance (for instance, the structures adopted by individuals and organizations to manage transactions). National institutions that impose greater constraints and monitoring on decision-makers in state-owned multinational enterprises are particularly important in this regard. A high degree of control, a highly developed legal system and high levels of capital market development have been proven to reduce the home market bias of state-owned multinational enterprises, thus driving them to develop strategies more similar to those of their private counterparts and making them, overall, more efficient (Cuervo-Cazurra et al., 2014).

On the other hand, from the perspective of external stakeholders, state-owned multinational companies represent a delicate counterpart for interaction. The diffusion of mixed state and private ownership, moreover, has made it more difficult to ascertain when the aims and actions of a state-owned firm are dictated by its public or its private "soul". Private competitors usually consider these companies a threat, accusing them of unfair competition because the government can help them in many ways, for instance, by creating a favorable framework for action, or by providing financial support, or via several other forms of aid that could include preferential regulatory treatment, state-backed guarantees or direct subsidies.

State-owned multinational companies, however, do not represent an issue only in terms of their foreign competitors abroad. Overall, suspicion of state-owned multinational companies remains great. Their very existence and legitimacy also generate concerns in other external players. Foreign countries could, for example, consider state-owned multinational companies a serious threat; these companies are still, in many cases, considered as tools created to achieve ideological and political aims. Consequently, they are seen as actors who might want to interfere in other sovereign countries to serve their home country's foreign policy, or else as a way to import technological developments from abroad.

On top of this, some state-owned multinationals certainly have a political dimension. This is the case with energy companies; despite a very internationalized business environment, these have kept a remarkable level of state ownership and have developed advanced systems that allow governments to successfully exercise their control over most national oil company governance systems. In a similar way, other key assets for the global economy are also under the ownership and control of governments and state-owned multinationals, such as the rare earth elements essential in clean energy production, electric vehicles, consumer electronics, national defense and more. China is by far the world's largest producer of these crucial assets, mainly through companies like the China Northern Rare Earth Group and the China Rare Earth Group, which are currently under the control of a state-owned holding: the State-owned Assets Supervision and Administration Commission of the State Council.

State-owned multinational companies, like private multinational firms, are therefore major players in current global dynamics at both the economic and geopolitical levels. They emerged from the economic context provided by the new international framework that developed since the last decades of the 20th century, when governments opened up markets because competition was considered a key instrument in improving the domestic economy. However, while the traditional model of state-owned enterprise originally acted as a national safeguard against the outside world, the state-owned companies of today can be considered a vital component of globalization, investing heavily across borders, sometimes in sectors and countries that private firms have neglected. They pursue a delicate balance in international relations and geopolitical dynamics, thus forging new global dynamics.

References

Jean-Pierre Anastassopoulos, George Blanc, and Pierre Dussage, *State-Owned Multinationals*. New York: John Wiley & Sons, 1987.

Garry D. Bruton, Mike W. Peng, David Ahlstrom, Ciprian Stan, and Kehan Xu, "State-owned enterprises around the world as hybrid organizations", *Academy of Management Perspectives*, 29(1), 2015: 92–114.

L. Jeremy Clegg, Hinrich Voss, and Janja A. Tardios, "The autocratic advantage: Internationalization of state-owned multinationals", *Journal of World Business*, 53(5), 2018: 668–681.

Judith Clifton, Francisco Comín, and Daniel Díaz Fuentes, *Privatisation in the European Union: Public Enterprises and Integration*. New York: Springer-Verlag, 2013.

Álvaro Cuervo-Cazurra, *State-Owned Multinationals: Governments in Global Business*. London: Palgrave-Macmillan, 2017.

Álvaro Cuervo-Cazurra, Andrew Inkpen, Aldo Musacchio, and Kennan Ramaswamy, "Governments as owners: State-owned multinational companies", *Journal of International Business Studies*, 45, 2014, 919–942.

Álvaro Cuervo-Cazurra and Cheng Li, "The internationalization of state-owned firms: Within country drivers", in Mike Wright, Geoffrey T. Wood, Alvaro Cuervo Cazurra, Pei Sun, Ilya Okhmatovskiy, and Anna Grosman (eds.), *The Oxford Handbook of State Capitalism and the Firm*. Oxford: Oxford University Press, 2022: 285.

John H. Dunning and Robert D. Pearce, *The World's Largest Industrial Enterprises 1962-1983*. Aldershot: Gower Publishing Company Ltd. V, 186, S, 1985.

Global SWF, *Sovereign Wealth Funds Report*, January 1, 2021.

Sergio G. Lazzarini, Luiz F. Mesquita, Felipe Monteiro, and Aldo Musacchio, "Leviathan as an inventor: An extended agency model of state-owned versus private firm invention in emerging and developed economies", *Journal of International Business Studies*, 52(4), 2020: 560–594.

Natalia Manuilova, Ruxandra Burdescu, and Anna Bilous, "State-owned enterprises during a crisis: Assets or liabities?", April 6th, 2022, World Bank Blogs.

Robert Millward, *Private and Public Enterprise in Europe: Energy, Telecommunications and Transport, 1830–1990*. Cambridge: Cambridge University Press, 2005.

Aldo Musacchio and Sergio G. Lazzarini, *Reinventing State Capitalism: Leviathan in Business, Brazil and Beyond*. Cambridge: Harvard University Press, 2014.

Aldo Musacchio, Felipe Monteiro, and Sergio G. Lazzarini, "State-owned multinationals in international competition", in Robert Grosse and Klaus Meyer (eds.), *The Oxford Handbook of Management in Emerging Markets*. Oxford: Oxford University Press, 2018: 569–590.

Pierangelo Toninelli, *The Rise and Fall of State-Owned Enterprise in the Western World*. Cambridge: Cambridge University Press, 2000.

World Bank, "*Bureaucrats in Business*", New York: Oxford University Press, 1995.

UNCTAD 2017, *Unctad, World Investment Report 2017.* Geneva: United Nations Publications, 2018.

UNCTAD 2019, *Unctad, World Investment Report, 2019.* Geneva: United Nations Publications, 2020.

Gaspar Vitor, Paulo Medas, and John Ralyea, "State-owned enterprises in the time of COVID-19", May 7h, 2020, IMF Blog.

Chapter 7

From globalization to fragmentation

FROM THE END TO THE BEGINNING OF HISTORY

7.1 "Globalization is almost dead"

On 6 December 2022, a symbolic event took place in Phoenix, Arizona. Morris Chang, the legendary father of Taiwan's semiconductor industry and founder of the powerful Taiwan Semiconductor Manufacturing Corporation (TSMC), was giving a celebratory speech at a new plant for advanced chip production which the Taiwanese undisputed market leader was going to open in the US town. This was two decades after the company's first investment overseas, in Camas, Washington State. Beside the ritual celebration, the speech reached a dramatic climax when Dr. Chang, referring to the global semiconductor industry but clearly speaking in general, openly delivered a dry epitaph for the global integration process that had characterized all the decades following the Cold War: "Twenty-seven years have passed and [the semiconductor industry] witnessed a big change in the world, a big geopolitical change in the world," Chang said. "*Globalization is almost dead and free trade is almost dead. A lot of people still wish they would come back, but I don't think they will be back* (emphasis added).[1] Chang's words could not have been more shocking, and for some good reasons.

Morris Chang is himself a living "product" of the present globalization wave. Born in 1931, he spent his early life in Civil War-torn China, emigrating at the beginning of the 1950s to the US. After graduating from the Massachusetts Institute of Technology (MIT), Chang started a 25-year career in the semiconductor division of Texas Instruments. In a world that allowed the free circulation of technological knowledge, Chang returned to Taiwan at the end of the Cold War and became a government advisor in charge of fostering the island

DOI: 10.4324/9780429490255-7

nation's technological development. In 1987, he founded his most important creation, TSMC, which quickly became the world leader in high-tech semiconductor production. TSMC made its outstanding market ascent (and its founder's fortune) thanks to the unique architecture of the global market for semiconductors, a shining example of a value chain spread across the globe. At present, TSMC is a key link in a complex and fragmented chain of production that has so far been based on semiconductor design (mostly in the US and Europe), machine tool producers (in the US) and "foundries" (mainly located in Taiwan), which are factories producing tailored semiconductors for customers all over the world. The human capital (electronic engineers and physicists) on which "semiconductor island" relies are the fruits of another global circuit of cultural exchanges, typically graduates from California or MIT.

The model described above, the so-called "fab-less" model, has so far accounted for more than half the world's semiconductor production. Even companies that design and produce their own semiconductors, such as Intel, often make use of TSMC's services because of its outstanding degree of technological advancement, not to mention its famed discretion.

Chang's personal history and experience make his words even more laden with significance. TSMC's leader was not simply referring to the turmoil that has engulfed and distorted the global market for semiconductors since 2019, when the Trump administration issued the so-called "Huawei ban", targeting the Chinese telecom champion's penetration of the US markets, and Western markets in general, with its 5G equipment. The death of globalization that Chang referred to was something more general and – in a true sense – "global".

7.2 Measuring globalization's *malaise*

Chapter 3 presented a series of indexes that "measure" various aspects of the global process of integration. Notwithstanding their differences in structure, parameters and variables, all unanimously confirm that the present globalization trend shows all the signs of a progressive slowdown, if not of a decline. For the purpose of this chapter, one of the indexes mentioned in Chapter 3, the KOF Globalisation Index, appears particularly useful. Not only does it include measurements of economic integration and trade, but it also covers other relevant dimensions of globalization; in particular it includes social, cultural and political dimensions, distinguishing between the *de facto* flows and exchanges, in terms of volumes, and the *de jure* conditions that allow these flows to take place: in other words, the ease of exchanges. The KOF Index shows a very similar trend for any indicator (see Chapter 3 for details), as can easily be seen along the time span for which the index is available, the 50-year period from 1970 to 2020. Although monotonic in shape (since the 1970s, the process of integration has indisputably accelerated at a global level), the trend shown in the index can be divided into three sections. The first, from 1970 to 1990, shows a moderate growth trend of the globalization variables, clearly implying a dynamic of moderate "regional globalization" starting immediately after the Second World War. A second section lasts from 1990 to 2008, the year of the global financial crisis; the curve now rises more clearly, suggesting an acceleration in the integration process, translating into two decades of hyper-globalization. From 2008 up to the present, however, the curve is once again relatively moderate. In the case of some components of the general index (particularly "social globalization" and "economic globalization), the derivate of the curve is already negative around 2015, well before the devastation of the COVID-19 pandemic. On the KOF website, one can watch a video with an evocative title: "Is Globalisation at Its End?"[2] If the available quantitative evidence clearly supports the idea of at least a significant and structural slowdown in the process of global integration, the experts' opinions are more nuanced, even if, in substance, almost everyone agrees that all the signs point toward a slowdown in the degree of global integration. While some prefer to use the term slow-balization, others, more pessimistically and openly, use the term de-globalization. A few optimists, such as the Director General of the World Trade Organization (WTO), Ngozi-Okonjo Iweala, in a recent article published in *Foreign Affairs*,[3] do recognize the problems, but openly suggest "reimagining" globalization. Instead of abandoning it, they cite the evidence of a global merchandise trade that "hit record levels in 2022", thanks to the fact that international commerce is still positively influenced by multilateral agreements. Intermediate inputs continue to flow intensely, which for the moment casts doubts on the alleged reshoring of global value chains. In any case, this optimism collides with a scenario in which the free flow of goods is increasingly subject to a growing number of restrictions and barriers, as suggested by the slowdown in *de jure* economic globalization reported in the KOF Index, and also in other pessimistic analyses of the effectiveness of institutions of global governance like the WTO.

However, the question that remains open is: what happened? What was the dynamic behind the reversal in the trend? What has made this process of integration, in which all those born in the 30-plus years since 1989 have lived their whole lives, turn into something that resembles its opposite? Another important question is: what will happen? And also: how long will this process of disintegration last? And, finally: are we equipped to pass from a global "World of Yesterday", to quote Austrian historian Stefan Zweig (see Chapter 2), into a situation that we still do not know, but which is very different?

Some of the answers to these questions can be no more than mere speculation, but some explanations can be proposed, and some historical parallels can be drawn. This will not enable us to perfectly forecast the future, but it will allow us to at least be conscious and prepared. The rest of this chapter will tentatively provide some explanations for the crisis of globalization, explicitly referring to what happened 150 years ago, when the first globalization, as described in Chapter 2, peaked, and then quickly turned into its opposite, precipitating the world into the hell of two world wars, one Great Depression, and a series of dictatorships and authoritarian regimes.

The thesis of this concluding chapter is that globalization is slowing down, or at worst is turning into its opposite, because the "gears" that over the last seven decades progressively kept the entire mechanism working are now suffering simultaneous structural problems. The next section will examine the "gears" of globalization, and the following section will explain what has caused them to jam.

7.3 The jammed gears

Chapters 1, 2 and 4 introduced, albeit briefly, the indispensable "gears" that allow a globalization wave to (re-)start, accelerate and reach its peak, in a process that so far has been shown as developing over a time span of several decades.

Chapter 4 described the most common accelerators of the spread of globalization: technological progress, institutional arrangements and cultural attitudes. It showed how these worked quite efficiently during the past and present globalization waves, moving the system toward consolidation of the globalization process. Chapters 1 and 2 suggested that these determinants (which for the moment can be labeled techno-socio-institutional) should be seen as accompanied by a number of other elements of a "political nature", which can in their turn condition the efficiency of the techno-socio-institutional drivers. The political elements can include those that are merely geopolitical, meaning the willingness of countries to keep or revise the established hierarchy of power, which in its turn affects the general climate of international relations. In addition, the nature of domestic politics introduces another important variable. It is no easy matter to establish a kind of hierarchy among these aspects that influence globalization. It is probably better to see all these elements as mutually interactive. As said above, the aim of this chapter is to analyze the nature and extent of the blockage in the mechanism.

7.3.1 Technological progress: from common good to global threat

As the previous chapters have clarified in detail, technological advancements, especially in transportation, information and communication technologies, were at the basis of the integration processes, both in the first and the second waves of globalization described in this book. One of the iconic images of the technological advancements that marked the second half of the 19th century is a famous lithograph published in 1876 as "The Progress of the Century – The Lightning Steam Press. The Electric Telegraph. The Locomotive. The Steamboat" (Figure 7.1). This image condenses all the positive messages of technological progress anticipated in Chapter 2; new transportation technologies represented by locomotives and steamships meant faster and cheaper connections and transportation of merchandise; improvements in printing technology allowed the circulation of news and information; and the electric telegraph (via an expanding network of cables on land and across the oceans) made it possible to connect distant places almost instantly. Steamships could also benefit from new trade routes and new infrastructures that made travel faster and easier. For instance, the opening of the Suez Canal in 1869, 45 years before the Panama Canal, allowed people and goods to travel

Figure 7.1 The progress of the century

"around" the world without having to circumnavigate continents. Progress was considered first and foremost as beneficial for mankind, as is written on the telegraph ribbon depicted in Figure 7.1: "LIBERTY AND UNION NOW AND FOREVER ONE AND INSEPARABLE. GLORY TO GOD IN THE HIGHEST. ON EARTH PEACE, GOOD WILL TOWARD MEN".

The inspirer of the Suez Canal was former French diplomat Ferdinand De Lesseps, whose aims included creating a "common" benefit for trade to be a driver of cooperation and peace between two powers that were historically hostile toward each other: France and Great Britain.

The power of technology as a driver of growth, cooperation and development followed the Second World War; the war actually enabled a number of technological innovations which in their turn supported the second wave of globalization, such as computers, the internet and commercial aviation. Technological progress allowing the intensification of trade flows and the rapid diffusion of information marked the 1950s. In one of those coincidences that are typical of history, 1956 saw both the invention of the container and the first functioning prototypes of silicon devices, or semiconductors (at Shockley Labs in northern California). Once again, trade and communication received a further boost from technological innovations, and these were rarely kept secret, as shown well by the fascinating story of Taiwanese specialization in semiconductor production.

To a certain extent, technological transfer – for which multinational enterprises were largely responsible – was considered a common benefit bringing growth and development where it was necessary, and allowing peripheral countries to accelerate a process of economic convergence. As recently noted by Miami-based management scholar Yadong Luo (Luo, 2022), the traditional version of techno-nationalism sees technology as an instrument promoting development and connectedness, which has particularly allowed Western multinationals to prosper after the Second World War. However, as Luo notes, the current version of techno-nationalism has been progressively transformed into its opposite, and is instead an "emerging strain of geopolitical thinking and actions that links technological capabilities directly to a country's national security and geopolitical benefits, involves legal and regulatory restrictions or sanctions against selected foreign investors or foreign companies", and it could be added, also against foreign governments considered hostile and dangerous. In sum, neo-techno-nationalism "mingles deeply and intricately with geopolitics, propelling a new time of worldwide de-globalization and decoupling with structural changes"; it interferes deeply with the action of companies and also with the wellbeing of the global economy. From being an agent of development, control over critical technologies is becoming a powerful weapon necessary to keep geopolitical competitors at bay. This can take the form of trade wars focusing on high-tech industries, as in the case of semiconductor production for artificial intelligence and quantum computing, as well as other symbolic events. In early 2023, a consortium known as Southeast-Asia Japan 2 or SJC2, involving the US firm Meta, Singapore Telecom and KDDI, Japan's second largest telecommunications company, ran into problems. The consortium was created in order to lay a 10,500-kilometer fiber-optic submarine communication cable between Singapore and Japan, with extensions to Mainland China, Taiwan and Hong Kong, but then the Chinese authorities raised security concerns in China's self-declared territorial waters of the South China Sea.

The words of an industry veteran, quoted by Nikkei Asia, well describe how the force of technology has quickly transformed into a geopolitical problem, in contrast with the situation in the early 1860s when the connection of the Eurasian and American continents was not seen as a political issue: "the challenges facing the business have changed quite a fair bit in recent years. *We all wish that it was the good old days, where we just come together and focus on connecting the world for global trade*" (emphasis added).[4] While the construction of the Suez Canal was a humanitarian nightmare for the enslaved local workers, it was welcomed as one of the wonders of the century, considerably shortening sea travel; it connected colonies to motherlands and allowed characters like Phileas Fogg to travel around the world at a speed unimaginable only a decade before the canal's opening. Also important was that the canal was built via peaceful collaboration between the French and the British Empire.

Today, a similar infrastructural initiative, aimed at connecting the Eurasian continent through a set of linkages and corridors – the Chinese-led and much-celebrated Belt and Road Initiative – is increasingly viewed in the West with suspicion and hostility, seen as an instrument for expanding Chinese influence and soft power. In sum, this is another battlefield in the ongoing clash between a challenger and the incumbent power (the West, collectively). In this perspective, the US appears particularly active, and also successful, in blocking Chinese participation in international projects regarding infrastructural connections and technological support of global integration, even at the cost of damaging its own national champions.

As reported by the *Financial Times* in a detailed 2023 infographics,[5] US companies like Meta and Amazon have planned since 2018 to lay cable networks across the Pacific, initially with the collaboration of China Mobile, which is a reason why Washington blocked the project. In 2021, they restarted the project without the Chinese, only to see the project blocked once again (with millions of dollars uselessly sinking into the Pacific). Moreover, the Chinese have not remained idle, and are engaged in connection projects with "friendly" countries, so that the logical consequence will most likely be a bifurcation of the global communication network, replicating the concept of decoupling, but in two distinct communication blocs. What has been correctly defined by *The Economist* in a recent analysis as "digital protectionism" is increasingly a reality.[6]

7.3.2 The crisis of the institutions of global governance

As introduced in Chapter 4, the second pillar of the present globalization is a set of global governance institutions that have been designed in roughly two stages: the first at Bretton Woods at the end of the Second World War, the second at the end of the Cold War with the emergence of the so-called "Washington Consensus".

In 2024, when this book is published, 80 years will have passed since the Bretton Woods Agreement, the spirit of which was to design a set of quite simple rules of behavior (technically, "institutions"). In contrast with the "dark valley" of authoritarian and nationalist autarky of the previous decades, another attitude was necessary; this was well summarized in the words of US Treasury secretary Henry Morgenthau, Jr. in the closing address of the three-week conference on 22 July 1944: "We have to come to recognize that the wisest and most effective way to protect our national interests is through international co-operation – that is to say, through united effort for the attainment of common goals" (US Department of State, 1944). In just a few effective sentences, Morgenthau expressed what can be considered as the birth certificate of the liberalist approach in international relations, also implicitly putting an end to the decades of selfish realism when national geopolitical interests prevailed over international cooperation, leading to two disastrous world conflicts in the space of only 25 years.

At Bretton Woods, some of the world's most important institutional agreements were designed. These included the General Agreement on Tariffs and Trade (GATT, merged with the World Trade Organization in 1995), aimed at making international trade easier, smoother and more stable, and other cooperative agreements related to monetary and economic policy, such as the International Monetary Fund (IMF) and a global development bank, the World Bank. This set the stage for other cooperative efforts to pool resources in support of regional development, such as the Asian Development Bank (founded in 1966) and the more recent Chinese-inspired Asian Infrastructure Investment Bank established in 2016.

In a very well-documented 2019 article,[7] the chief economic commentator of the authoritative *Financial Times*, Martin Wolf, summarizes the unquestionable results of those brand-new rules of cooperative behavior: long-term stability of the global economy, an overall decline in the percentage of people living in extreme poverty, coupled with a parallel increase in living standards, particularly in Asia, and for several decades there was also monetary stability. This stability was due to the system of fixed exchange rates comparable only to the Gold Standard system underpinning the global integration of the second half of the 19th century. Overall, at the end of the Cold War, these institutions had reached full maturity, and supported by the rare unipolar moment, they offered a launch pad for the present hyper-globalization phase. In the end, these institutions were all physically based in Washington, DC to further boost (perhaps excessively) the process of liberalization, privatization and democratization that had characterized the opening of the new millennium.

As in the case of technology, however, almost all the institutions designed at Bretton Woods are now suffering an apparently unavoidable decay, a "dysfunction", as was acutely noted by international policy expert Uri Dadush in an article published in 2014.[8]

Cooperation on trade is in tatters: multilateral agreements increasingly side-step the WTO as a generally agreed institution. The reason is relatively simple: friendly countries tend to create conventions "*ad excludendum*", aimed at excluding from international agreements those countries considered dangerous, for what are basically political reasons.

Similarly, the IMF is now under heavy criticism, particularly among the countries of the Global South, for its rigid attitude toward inflation control and fiscal adjustments. The Asian crisis of the late 1990s and the global financial distress of 2007 have clearly highlighted the flaws of an institution that incentivized the accumulation of foreign exchange reserves by states outside the group of "rich countries". However, more importantly, as reported in a recent article published by *The Economist*,[9] the (once) fundamental pillar of global macroeconomic stability (in almost 80 years since its creation, the IMF has lent $700 billion to 150 countries) faces at least three important threats. The first of these is that China, now one of the world's main creditors, is reluctant to write off loans to poor countries just to allow the US-influenced IMF step in as lender, while the IMF does not intend to lend to countries indebted to China just to see the funds flow into China. The second threat is that a group of middle-income countries that regularly turn to the IMF do not appear capable of using the fund's money to make progress, despite a continuous succession of bail-out and financing programs; still, the IMF has to be there in some form for geopolitical reasons, in order to keep Chinese money at bay. Finally, the IMF is struggling with a sort of path dependence impeding use of its funds to address some of the "global challenges" (for instance, global warming). All in all, it appears clear that two out of the three reasons for the IMF's enfeeblement have to be connected to a shaky geopolitical scenario. As the article clearly suggests, "Like many liberal institutions built after the Second World War that could both serve American interests and claim to represent all of humanity, the fund is now ensnared by the Sino-American rivalry."

No less serious are the troubles of another Bretton Woods' creation, the World Bank. Once the sole, unchallenged development bank, it has been progressively sidelined by other similar institutions in which US control has rapidly declined. If the Asian Development Bank is still firmly controlled by the US and Japan, alternatives have now multiplied. The BRICS Development Bank (now the New Development Bank) was established in 2015 to support infrastructure and sustainable development projects, and counts among its founding members Brazil, Russia, India, China and South Africa, recently joined by Bangladesh, the United Arab Emirates and Egypt. There is no trace here of Western countries, least of all the US. Similarly, the Asian Infrastructure Investment Bank (AIIB), a self-declared multilateral institution with China as its largest blockholder, was founded in 2016 to finance projects of infrastructural connectivity in its member states. The AIIB has 47 "regional" members (the countries located in an "enlarged" version of Asia that includes the Middle East and Oceania), and another 45 non-regional members in Europe, Africa and the American Continent from north to south. Also in this case, the absence of the US is notable.

For a very long time – for about seven decades after the Second World War – the Bretton Woods institutions embodied a set of common and shared values belonging to the world's richest and most developed democracies (coinciding *de facto* with the Western countries). Good or bad, they successfully laid a reasonable foundation for the process of re-globalization that accelerated firstly into globalization and then after the end of the Cold War turned into an apparently unstoppable process of hyper-globalization. The set of liberal policies governing the post-Cold War globalization, known as the Washington Consensus can be seen, in the end, as the highpoint of the Bretton Woods institutions. However, globalization itself brought to the forefront a number of countries whose values, political constitutions, worldviews and expectations did not coincide with those of the creators of the post-Second World War institutions of global governance. This has brought crisis and disruption, with the consequence that another essential gear of globalization has inevitably jammed.

7.3.3 "Citizens of nowhere"

In October 2016, a few months after the Brexit referendum, British ex-prime minister Theresa May gave an extremely populist speech at the annual

Conservative Party conference. May was presenting her vision of Britain's bright future outside the European Union (EU), but above all, here was an opportunity to blame the EU (in the view of this book, one example of regional integration preceding the post-Cold War global integration) as the symbol of a world that worked well for a privileged happy few, but not for "the people", particularly after the 2007–2008 financial crisis. It was the ordinary citizens who paid the highest price of these situations, not the elites. As May put it effectively:

> if you're one of those people who lost their job, who stayed in work but on reduced hours, took a pay cut as household bills rocketed, or – and I know a lot of people don't like to admit this – someone who finds themselves out of work or on lower wages because of low-skilled immigration, life simply doesn't seem fair. It feels like your dreams have been sacrificed in the service of others.[10]

According to May's rhetoric, the elites living in wealthy London (one of the examples of a "Global City", an adamant product of globalization) had an additional fault: they had abdicated the values of their citizenship, their moral obligations toward their fellow citizens, since globalization allowed them "to take on cheap labor from overseas" instead of training up "local young people". In doing this, those in a position of power gave up their citizenship's moral obligation in order to become part of an international elite, radically different from the "people down the road". Then, in a perfect and effective example of populist rhetoric, May added a sentence which sparked both criticism and enthusiastic support: "But if you believe you're a citizen of the world, you're a citizen of nowhere. You don't understand what the very word 'citizenship' means."

May's speech mixed many issues that are key arguments in this chapter: populism, the globalization backlash, the resurgence of nationalism and of local interests. Above all, however, in May's triumphant rhetoric, what resounded was an aggressive cultural critique of globalization; the expression "citizen of nowhere" contained the negation of one of the cultural underpinnings of globalization, a badge that had been proudly displayed by intellectuals like Stefan Zweig (see Chapter 2): cosmopolitanism.

A third jammed gear is the cultural support for globalization as a beneficial process in social, cultural and economic terms. In this section, we intend not simply to discuss the critique of cultural globalization. The argument is different: what is in default is the concept of globalization as a positive win–win process from several different points of view. Several scholars have defined this as the "globalization backlash", indicating a decline in policy support for globalization.

Cultural acceptance of the recent wave of globalization can be roughly divided into two periods: the post-Cold War decades of accelerated integration until the 2008 financial crisis, and then the period after the crisis. Apart from some underground criticism, globalization was considered promising during the two decades after the Berlin Wall came down, and in several cases it provided a bright future for the countries and people involved in it.

The pervasive, intense and extended benefits of global trade were felt at the level of the economic systems of both advanced and developing countries. The symbols of this process were the foundation in 1995 of the WTO, and China's entry to this multilateral global trade system, eagerly brokered by the US. The acceleration of global trade not only provided economic opportunities, but other fruits were supposed to be in that cornucopia, namely the global diffusion of liberal democratic political regimes, and it was also supposed to bring peace after so many decades of international tension during the Cold War. For about three decades, the executives of the largest international companies were almost free to take their strategic decisions while forgetting political and geopolitical constraints, and they became increasingly used to this freedom. In a recent article published in June 2023 in *Foreign Affairs*, inequality scholar Branko Milanovic stresses how globalization maintained at least one of its promises.[11] On a global scale, the world of today is much more equal than it was a century ago. In Milanovic's words, global income inequality began to grow from the advent of the Industrial Revolution, mostly benefitting Western countries, whereas global inequality levels began to decline about two decades ago, thanks above all to the rise of China. According to Milanovic, the Gini index of global inequality peaked in 1988 at a level of 69.4, but dropped to 60.1 in 2018, "a level not seen since the end of the nineteenth century". This was, in sum, a situation that J.M. Keynes would have eagerly applauded in his introduction to *The Economic Consequences of the Peace* (see below; Keynes, 1920).

Now comes what caused the bitterness of Theresa May's speech. If globalization reduced global inequality now and during the second half of the 19th century, this was also thanks to the presence of empires with a global reach, like the British Empire, currently imploding into an island self-isolated from the global economy, to the joy of its Conservative populist leaders. Globalization has failed to at least keep inequality levels low inside countries, particularly in the once-rich Western countries. The truth, as Milanovic effectively states it, is that "non-Westerners with rising incomes will displace poor and middle-class Westerners from their lofty perches. Such a shift will underscore the polarization in rich countries, between those who are wealthy by global standards and those who are not". Here are the roots of the rage, and this is where the backlash against globalization lies.

7.4 The rot from within

Thus, several gears have begun to jam during the last decade. In order to better understand the dynamics and the tangible effects of this backlash, it is now useful to turn to another area of social sciences: politics. Here again, insights can be gained from the story of how the first globalization collapsed into its contrary, de-globalization, a planetary financial crisis, and a wave of authoritarianism and dictatorships in the "dark valley" of two world wars.

7.4.1 Grapes of wrath

In recent years, political scientists have published an increasing volume of qualitative and quantitative evidence concerning the relationship between globalization, the globalization backlash and the transformation in the domestic political landscape of countries affected by the backlash. In general, the direction of causality is relatively clear. As pointed out above, globalization is disruptive at the country level. The effect is particularly felt in some areas of the once-rich West. This has rapidly translated into a widespread sense of anger, very similar to that described in Pankai Mishra's book *The Age of Anger* (Mishra, 2018), which connected the increasing support for nationalist supremacism and populism around the world with a reaction to globalization's unfulfilled promises. It is quite significant that the opening chapter of Mishra's book explicitly refers to another "age of anger", the one that characterized the peak of the first globalization, which was marked by a spread of xenophobic nationalist ideologies across the West, targeting one of globalization's tangible symbols, foreign migrants, together with the ubiquitous free trade policies. This was an "anti-global shift", which matured before the First World War and exploded after it, as noted by Tara Zahra in her book *Against the World* (Zahra, 2023). Nationalism, populism and authoritarian regimes were – and not only in Europe – the political outcome of a cultural shift that saw hostility replace the amicable attitude to cosmopolitanism that had characterized the second half of the 19th century.

What constituted the ultimate determinant of this change of attitude is a matter of endless historical analysis.

A good starting point is J.M. Keynes' famous and oft-quoted description of the golden age of the global economy in the first chapter of his book *The Economic Consequences of the Peace* (Keynes, 1920, pp. 10–12)

What an extraordinary episode in the economic progress of man that age was which came to an end in August 1914! The greater part of the population, it is true, worked hard and lived at a low standard of comfort, yet were, to all appearances, reasonably contented with this lot. But escape was possible, for any man of capacity or character at all exceeding the average, into the middle and upper classes, for whom life offered, at a low cost and with the least trouble, conveniences, comforts, and amenities beyond the compass of the richest and most powerful monarchs of other ages. The inhabitant of London could order by telephone, sipping his morning tea in bed, the various products of the whole earth, in such quantity as he might see fit, and reasonably expect their early delivery upon his doorstep; he could at the same moment and by the same means adventure his wealth in the natural resources and new enterprises of any quarter of the world, and share, without exertion, or even trouble, in their prospective fruits and advantages; or he could decide to couple the security of his fortunes with the good faith of the townspeople of any substantial municipality in any continent that fancy or information might recommend. He could secure forthwith, if he wished it, cheap and comfortable means of transit to any country or climate without passport or other formality, could dispatch his servant to the neighboring office of a bank for such supply of the precious metals as might seem convenient, and could then proceed abroad to foreign quarters, without knowledge of their religion, language, or customs, bearing coined wealth upon his person, and would consider himself greatly aggrieved and much surprised at the least interference. But, most important of all, he regarded this state of affairs as normal, certain, and permanent.

This long and fascinating description of a lost age is interesting for two reasons. Of course, one is its similarity to our present, and Keynes' terms can easily be replaced with ones we are familiar with: "telephone" with "internet", "delivery" with "Amazon" and "neighboring office of a bank" with "ATM". The second reason lies in his opening sentence, sometimes omitted in quotations of this extract:

The greater part of the population, it is true, worked hard and lived at a low standard of comfort, yet were, to all appearances, reasonably contented with this lot.

The key question, here is exactly this: were they really *reasonably contented?* The first globalization promoted global economic efficiency in a context of (relative) peace, guaranteed by a stable geopolitical world order under British dominance. However, it was unable to prevent the spread of income inequality and had challenged social cohesion and equilibrium, particularly in Western societies. US analyst Ward Wilson, published an article in *Foreign Policy* in 2014, on the hundredth anniversary of the outbreak of the First World War, with the telling title "The Age of Frustration".[12] In this, he described the widespread sense of anger and desperation that culminated in extreme nationalism and widespread violence. This ultimately brought acceptance of war as an antidote to the stifling peace that had permeated Europe for almost a century since Napoleon's death. In his own words, the period preceding the war:

> was called the Belle Époque by those lucky enough to be the wealthy of Europe – a time of top hats, ennui, and stately promenading. [...] While the upper classes felt ennui during "the beautiful age," others felt a dangerous sense of desperation.

And for many good reasons. According to available data, inequality levels in Western countries grew during the second half of the 19th century up until the outbreak of the First World War. As said above, inequality fostered anti-globalism, which then took the shape of nationalism and support for populist governments before and after the conflict.

And today? According to the most recent research available, the globalization backlash has had a direct effect on the rising consensus for populist parties (both right- and left-wing) that has spread across the entire West during the last decade. Databases are abundant and generally convergent in showing how the countries and regions mostly affected by the negative redistributive effects of global integration are those where there is stronger support for populist parties, and in the case of Europe, also for "Eurosceptic" political groups. In its most extreme version, as recently suggested by *The Economist*, there is a troubling relationship between authoritarianism and globalization.[13]

It is not easy to understand the characteristics of populist parties due to differences in situations. Populism combines several elements of left- and right-wing ideologies, but its primary and most effective message is that the people have a "moral" superiority over the elites. Of course, the people are normally intended as the population of the country, as opposed to "foreigners" like migrants. As they did a century and a half ago, the vast majority of today's Western populist parties tend to mix supremacist and nationalist ideologies (if leaning to the right or far right), or anti-capitalist and statist tendencies (if leaning to the left or far left). In Western countries, both Europe and the US, the rise of populism has largely – but not exclusively – meant support for right-wing, nationalist, Eurosceptic parties. While not all populist parties openly oppose globalization, once in power they tend to favor the "people" via protectionist policies; an example is Donald Trump's policy toward China and more generally toward multilateral trade agreements, which were systematically suspended or even cancelled. Here again, nothing is new: the political reaction to the first globalization was a poisonous "mix" of xenophobic nationalism, populist propaganda and widespread protectionist tendencies. All in all, there is a global rise in illiberalism, as acutely (and recently) noted by political scientists Alexander Cooley and Daniel Nexon in a thoughtful article published in *Foreign Affairs*.[14]

7.4.2 *When geopolitics jumps in*

However, the populist reaction against globalization is just one of the political consequences of global integration. Another series of consequences concerns another level of politics, that of international relations and of geopolitical (dis-)equilibria.

Praising the achievements of globalization in the article already mentioned, Branko Milanovic takes China as an example of a (perhaps excessively) successful driver of reduction in global inequality levels; in less than half a century since the phase of "reforms" inaugurated under Deng's leadership in 1978, China has successfully undertaken the path of income convergence. However, in this book's perspective it is not the Chinese convergence or that of other developing countries which is relevant, but the effects this has had on another of the gears that can advance or dramatically slow down the process of global integration. This is where the realm of international relations, and more precisely the impact of geopolitics, lies.

In an insightful article published in *Foreign Affairs* almost a decade ago,[15] international relations expert Walter Russell Mead explored the emergence of a number of what were then regional mid-sized powers aiming to challenge the unipolar status quo that had followed the end of the Cold War and the establishment of the so-called *Pax Americana*. In the article, Mead was not immediately interested in exploring the destiny of globalization. His main considerations concerned the change in the post-Cold War world order, and the willingness (or rather, strong desire) of emerging powers to challenge the position of the incumbent; in this case, the incumbent was primarily the US, and the West in general.

In a recent note published in *Foreign Affairs*, Mark Leonard,[16] current Director of the European Council on Foreign Relations, quotes an exchange between Chinese president Xi Jinping and Vladimir Putin: "Right now, there are changes – the likes of which we haven't seen for 100 years – and we are the ones driving these changes together." It would be difficult to find better words to describe what a "revisionist power" is and what it wants. According to Leonard, the Chinese leadership in particular has a very clear idea of what the next "geopolitical era" will be; it will be fundamentally different from the bipolar post-Second World War order and even more different from the post-Cold War order of *Pax Americana*. It will be dramatically similar to that of the interwar years, as a "multipolar order without a hegemon", a multipolar order in which China will, of course, have the status of a great power and thus definitively erase the century of great humiliation inflicted on it by the West.

What is it that links this impending "geopolitical shift" and the fate of globalization? China, Russia and other "revisionist powers" in the so-called Global South base their willingness to re-shape the current world order on various principles (revanchism against the West, strong nationalist tendencies, the desire to restore modern versions of glorious empires of the past), but also on a solid basis: the benefits globalization has brought their own national economies, as stressed by the Chinese leader in 2017 at the World Economic Forum in Davos.

In fact, global integration transformed China into a modern version of the "Workshop of the World", allowing the accumulation of enormous resources to invest in the aggrandizement of the country's status, its hard and soft power, its territorial claims and ultimately its aspirations to global leadership. At the same time, globalization made Russia, like other petrostates, the world's energy provider, allowing also in this case the accumulation of enormous foreign currency reserves. Returning to Milanovic's argument, globalization not only creates convergence in equality among countries, but geopolitically speaking, it also gives revisionist powers the resources they need to aspire to the status of great power and question the status quo. According to some (very pessimistic) commentators like Matthew Kroenig[17] , this is a significant case in which the concept of assertive realism in international relations is back, explaining the rising levels of geopolitical assertiveness.

Here again, history provides some interesting insights. During the phase of rampant globalization in the second half of the 19th century, one effect of global integration was undoubtedly the irresistible economic rise of Germany after its unification in 1871 and the birth of the Second Reich. This event began to disturb the peace established by the European Concert of Powers, questioning the geopolitical structure of multipolarity with a hegemon (the

UK), and quickly upsetting the continent's geopolitical equilibrium. It is not hazardous to draw some parallels with the present situation, with an incumbent hegemon facing an emerging challenger, as correctly noted by Martin Wolf – see Chapter 1).[18]

7.4.3 War by other means

The impact on the present global integration comes because the clash between incumbent and challenger (see Allison's *Thucydides' Trap*, mentioned in Chapter 1) is presently being fought "by other means", to borrow from a bestseller by US analysts Robert Blackwill and Jennifer Harris (Blackwill and Harris 2016). The book's message is quite simple: due to a combination of ideological reasons and understandable neglect, the US has never weaponized its economic power or its technological superiority. However, the same is not true in the case of the willing-to-be great revisionist powers, which have leveraged heavily on economic and technological variables to promote and defend their national interests, achieve beneficial geopolitical goals, limit other polities' reach, and not least in order of importance, in order to subjugate minor powers via their soft power; the obvious reference is of course to Chinese statecraft strategies. The subtitle of the book, "Geoeconomics and Statecraft", is not irrelevant, since it openly refers to the skill of managing state affairs, both domestic and international, as a result of geoeconomic strategies. Quoting the "inventor" of this neologism, US analyst Edward Luttwak in a seminal article,[19] geoeconomics is the explicit use of economic weapons to achieve geopolitical goals.

Blackwill and Harris' book is a political pamphlet; it contains a sharp strategy indication (among other strategies, the US must use geoeconomics if it wants to keep its leading position among the world powers) and a list of instruments (geoeconomic weapons) to use, which range from sanctions to cyberwarfare and other "amenities", including the above-mentioned neo-techno-nationalist practices.

It is of course no coincidence that a year after the publication of the book, some of these strategic suggestions were eagerly picked up and put into practice by the new and aggressive Trump administration, which embarked on a ruthless "war by other means" to keep China at bay in what is considered one of the most important battlefields for supremacy: the ongoing information and communication technology revolution, and in particular 5G communication systems, supercomputing and artificial intelligence. Nor has the present Biden-Harris administration adopted a more conciliatory attitude.

The US National Security Strategy for 2022 rests on many pillars, but three seem to fit particularly well with the scenario introduced above: the first is a more traditional geopolitical approach of "containment" of Chinese expansion through a revamped system of global alliance, particularly in the Indo-Pacific region. The second is the reinvigoration of the ideological/cultural struggle between autocratic regimes and liberal democracies. The third is an aggressive geoeconomic strategy based on control of crucial technologies, particularly in the semiconductor industry, and a reduction in the mutual interdependence of the US/Western and Chinese economies. This process of blocking global interconnections is now universally known as "decoupling strategy", tactically conducted through "reshoring" (when relocated domestically) or "friend-shoring" (when relocated in countries politically close) of investments and activities once located abroad, particularly in countries that are already (or likely to become) hostile (see Chapter 5). Returning to the start of this chapter, this is already a reality in some industries more than in others, and has severely disrupted sophisticated architectures of exchange like the global value chain in semiconductors mentioned above.

7.4.4 Possible futures

How much impact will this have on the status of the present globalization? Will this decoupling be complete? In theory, decoupling will lead to a situation like the Cold War, which, at least at the beginning, coincided basically with a partition of the world economy into two quasi-independent blocs, with the creation of independent currency systems, one based on the dollar/euro and the other on the renminbi. Or will it resemble a "selective partition" in which only some "non-strategic" industries will continue to enjoy a fully globalized world economy? Or will there be a combination of the two alternatives above, given that, as most observers and commentators agree, the world of today is extremely interdependent and, above all, unlike the Cold War geopolitical order, the West and China do not have the same weight in the global economy. According to Mark Leonard's commentary mentioned earlier, while the Western bloc plus the world accounted for nearly 90 percent of global GDP after the Second World War, thanks to Milanovic's Great Convergence their share is now less than 60 percent. This means that the destiny of the world order, and of the global economy, will not (perhaps fortunately) be decided exclusively in Washington and Beijing.

7.5. Squeezed in between

In short, the status of the present globalization can be seen metaphorically as a piece of solid material squeezed between two cylinders that rotate in opposite directions. At the end of the process, the shape of this material will be totally different.

One of the cylinders represents the threat to globalization posed by the jamming of several mechanisms that, after the tragedy of the Second World War, progressively allowed the reappearance of supra-regional economic, social and political spaces (for instance, the European Union), and then after the Chinese reforms, the end of the Cold War and the creation of the WTO progressively laid the foundations for a further acceleration of globalization, additionally boosted by the neoliberal vision of the Washington Consensus. The present globalization is, first of all, threatened by this general jamming of gears, which in its turn has its origins in the "globalization backlash", meaning a cultural rejection of globalization as fundamentally unable to deliver on what it promised: a cornucopia of equal possibilities for every citizen of the world. Those most threatened are the ones who live in the most advanced countries. Rising inequality is the *primum movens*, and is eagerly politicized by domestic populist movements, as noted by Swiss-based political scientist Stephanie Walter.[20]

The second rotating cylinder squeezing the present world of global integration has a different nature, although the engine moving it is the same. In this case, globalization comes under pressure for purely geopolitical reasons. Globalization increases inequality levels inside both advanced and less advanced countries. However, it also increases the opportunities for countries previously excluded from the world's control boardroom to advance their strategy of revision of the current world order. For the incumbents, the only way to keep these at bay, or at least to slow down the process, is to find a way to reduce the opportunities for these emerging powers to obtain enough resources (economic, financial and above all technological) to pursue their revisionist interests. Figure 7.2 attempts to reconstruct the interactions among the variables affecting the speed and pressure of the two rotating cylinders.

The result of this double pressure is presumably that globalization will take quite a different shape, transformed in its nature and its structure.

The parallel with the story of how the previous globalization wave transformed and ended is possible. However, it is the historian's duty to warn the reader that (fortunately) history never repeats, although as Mark Twain is credited with saying: "it rhymes".

In a forgotten article titled "The Rivalry of Germany and England", published in *The Sewanee Review* in April 1913, US historian Edward Raymond Turner,[21] at the end of his career as Professor of European History at Johns Hopkins University in Baltimore, Maryland gave a plain and objective description of Germany's economic rise to become an unquestionably major power in

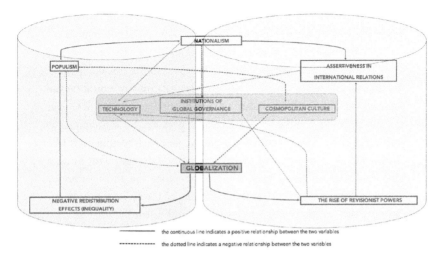

Figure 7.2 The jammed gears of globalization squeezed by the cylinder of inequality/populism/nationalism and the cylinder of nationalism/assertiveness/geopolitical revisionism

continental Europe before and after its political unification. Turner explicitly mentioned the integration of markets which had made the fortune of Britain's economy and power, and Germany's steady increase in strength due to its excellence in the industries of the Second Industrial Revolution. The relations between the two powers, the one incumbent and the other emerging, could have been peaceful for the sake of mutual interest. In fact, this was actually the case for some time, until Germany decided to invest its excess resources in military spending, and specifically in building a navy to rival Britain's. Although Turner does not use the term, this was the moment when geopolitical rivalry jumped in, worsened by the demographic expansion of Germany, with a population that would soon be double that of Great Britain. In sum, the cylinder of geopolitics began to rotate at increasing speed. Turner's conclusion is straightforward and dramatically prophetic:

> And so at last it had come to this, that the two greatest nations of Europe, the two which should be the leaders of its civilization, were in deadly antagonism, with each thinking most about its rival. From the Atlantic, from the Mediterranean, from the China seas, England had drawn her war fleets in an ever-increasing cordon around the British Isles. Feverishly new ships were being constructed; zealously new naval bases were prepared. All of

this was avowedly against Germany. And beyond the North Sea millions of German artisans and peasants were paying hunger taxes to build fleets against England. What would be the outcome of this? A war between the two would be a world disaster, incalculable in its horror and destruction, while not less calamitous would be the obliteration of England under a triumphant German civilization. As the historian reaches the immediate present, he cannot pierce the veil before him except by prophecy, and such prophecy is idle and fruitless. Nevertheless, whatever comes, it may well be that future writers looking back will declare that the most ominous thing in European politics at the beginning of the twentieth century was the dangerous rivalry of Germany and England.

After about a year, there was no longer any need for prophecies. The first global economy had finally imploded into de-globalization and fragmentation. The veil was pierced without remedy: behind it lay 20 million deaths and the prospect of around three decades of violent authoritarian dictatorships, the darkness of isolation, autarky and assertive aggressiveness. Finally, there arrived another global conflict that was even more devastating.

For the present, this is a serious lesson. However, as with each history lesson, the importance of knowledge of the past is that it gives at least a chance to avoid the worst.

Notes

1 Cheng Ting-Fang, "TSMC Founder Morris Chang Says Globalization 'Almost Dead'", *Nikkei Asia*, December 7, 2022.
2 https://www.youtube.com/watch?v=MydLsDzUAzY, accessed December 2023.
3 Ngozi-Okonyo Iweala, "Why The World Still Needs Trade", *Foreign Affairs*, Vol. 102, Issue 4, July/August 2023, pp. 94–103.
4 Tsubasa Suruga, "Asia's Internet Cable Projects Delayed by South China Sea Tensions", *Nikkei Asia*, May 19, 2023.
5 "How the US Is Pushing China Out of the Internet Plumbing", *Financial Times*, June 13, 2023, https://ig.ft.com/subsea-cables/, accessed December 2023.
6 "In Asia Data Flows Are Part of a New Great Game. Geopolitical Tension and Digital Protectionism Threaten to Undermine a More Connected Region", *The Economist*, July 10, 2023.
7 Martin Wolf, "Martin Wolf on Bretton Woods at 75: Global Co-operation under Threat", *Financial Times*, July 10, 2019.
8 Uri Dadush, "The Decline of Bretton Woods Institutions", *The National Interest*, September 22, 2014.

9 "The IMF Faces a Nightmarish Identity Crisis", *The Economist*, April 4, 2023.

10 "Theresa May: I'll Use Power of State to Build Fairer Britain", *BBC News*, October 5, 2016, https://www.bbc.com/news/uk-politics-37556019, accessed December 2023.

11 Branko Milanovic, "The Great Equality and Its Discontents", *Foreign Affairs*, Vol. 102, Issue 4, July/August 2023, pp. 78–93.

12 Ward Wilson, "The Age of Frustration", *Foreign Policy,* November 13, 2014.

13 "Globalization and Autocracy Are Locked Together. For How Much Longer? Disentangling the Two Will Be Hard, and Costly", *The Economist*, March 2022.

14 Alexander Cooley and Daniel H. Nexon, "The Real Crisis of the Global Order: Illiberalism on the Rise." *Foreign Affairs*, January/February 2022, pp. 103–118.

15 Walter Russell Mead, "The Return of Geopolitics: The Revenge of the Revisionist Powers", *Foreign Affairs*, Vol. 93, Issue 3, May/June 2014, pp. 69–79.

16 Mark Leonard, "China Is Ready for a World of Disorder. America Is Not", *Foreign Affairs*, Vol. 102, Issue 4, July/August 2023, pp. 116–127.

17 Matthew Krenig, "International Relations Theory Suggests That Great-Powers War Is Coming", *Foreign Policy*, August 27, 2022.

18 Martin Wolf, "Unsettling Precedents for Today's World", *Financial Times*, October 26, 2019.

19 Edward Luttwak, "From Geopolitics to Geo-economics: Logic of Conflict, Grammar of Commerce", *The National Interest*, Summer 1990, pp. 17–23.

20 Stephanie Walter, "The Backlash against Globalization, *Annual Review of Political Sciences*, Vol. 24, Issue 2021, pp. 421–442.

21 Edward Raymond Turner, "The Rivalry of Germany and England", *The Sewanee Review*, Vol. 21, Issue 2, 1913, pp. 129–147.

References

Robert D. Blackwill, Jennifer M. Harris, *War by Other Means: Geoeconomics and Statecraft*, Cambridge (Mass.): Belknap Press, 2016.

John Maynard Keynes, *The Economic Consequences of the Peace*, New York: Harcourt, Brace and Howe, 1920.

Yadong Luo, "Illusions of techno-nationalism". *Journal of Inernational Business Studies*, 53, 2022: 550–567.

Pankai Mishra, *The Age of Anger*, London: Allen Lane, 2018.

US. Department of State (ed.). *United Nations Monetary and Financial Conference: Bretton Woods, Final Act and Related Documents, New Hampshire, July 1 to July 22, 1944*, Washington: United States Government Printing Office, 1944.

Tara Zahra, *Against the World. Anti-Globalism and Mass Politics Between the World Wars*, New York: W. W. Norton Co, 2023.

Index

Note: Page numbers in *italics* indicate figures, **bold** indicate tables in the text

For Product Safety Concerns and Information please contact our EU
representative GPSR@taylorandfrancis.com
Taylor & Francis Verlag GmbH, Kaufingerstraße 24, 80331 München, Germany

www.ingramcontent.com/pod-product-compliance
Ingram Content Group UK Ltd.
Pitfield, Milton Keynes, MK11 3LW, UK
UKHW021844240425
457818UK00007B/279